Monism Matters

Monism Matters

The Significance of Type Monism for the Mind-Body Debate

TORIN ALTER

OXFORD
UNIVERSITY PRESS

Great Clarendon Street, Oxford, OX2 6DP,
United Kingdom

Oxford University Press is a department of the University of Oxford.
It furthers the University's objective of excellence in research, scholarship,
and education by publishing worldwide. Oxford is a registered trade mark of
Oxford University Press in the UK and in certain other countries.

Published in the United States of America by Oxford University Press
198 Madison Avenue, New York, NY 10016, United States of America.

British Library Cataloguing in Publication Data
Data available

Library of Congress Control Number: 2026934868

ISBN 9780198931539 (pbk.)
ISBN 9780198932390 (hbk.)

DOI: 10.1093/9780198931560.001.0001

Printed and bound by
CPI Group (UK) Ltd., Croydon, CR0 4YY

The manufacturer's authorized representative in the EU for product safety is
Oxford University Press España S.A. of Parque Empresarial San Fernando de Henares,
Avenida de Castilla, 2 – 28830 Madrid (www.oup.es/en or product.safety@oup.com).
OUP España S.A. also acts as importer into Spain of products made by the manufacturer.

In memory of my parents:
Irving Joseph Alter and Janet Kramer Alter

Contents

Acknowledgments

Robert J. Howell and I planned to co-write this book. Although that did not happen, it would be difficult to overstate his influence, and I cannot thank him enough. I am indebted to him, Sam Coleman, Russell Daw, Rebecca Kerley, Derk Pereboom, and Leopold Stubenberg for detailed, insightful comments on the entire manuscript. For valuable suggestions, I am grateful to Christopher Devlin Brown, William J. FitzPatrick, Amy Kind, Adam Pautz, A. Houston Smit, and three anonymous OUP referees.

I gave presentations on related topics at The Alabama Philosophical Society, Melissa Ebbers's Mind and Language Work-in-Progress Zoom Group, and Philosophy Departments at Indiana University Bloomington, Rice University, The University of Alabama, The University of Delaware, and The University of Mississippi. I thank those in attendance for their helpful feedback. I thank The University of Alabama for a sabbatical during which I wrote the first draft. Many ideas came to me while on daily walks with my pug Otter and his brother Scout. I thank them and my children, Dora and Irving, for inspiration. I thank my OUP editors, Peter Momtchiloff, Jamie Mortimer, and April Peake, for their patience and support. Finally, I thank my first and best philosophy professor, Jay Garfield. My intellectual and personal debt to him runs deep.

Chapters 1, 3, and 4 draw from "Physicalism, supervenience, and monism" (Alter and Howell 2022). Chapter 4 also draws from "A defense of the supervenience requirement on physicalism" (Alter 2021). Chapter 5 draws from "Physicalism and fundamental mentality" (Alter 2024).

Introduction

1. Main thesis

The concrete world contains a great diversity of phenomena. There are quarks, molecules, trees, wombats, persons, Nerf balls, nations, galaxies, and more. The properties those entities have, and the relations in which they stand, are no less varied. But is there an underlying commonality—a fundamental nature that everything shares? That is the question of monism. Or at least, it is *a* question of monism, which has intrigued philosophers for millennia.

This book's main thesis is that considerations about monism figure importantly in the contemporary mind-body debate. In short, *monism matters.* To some philosophers, this monism-matters thesis will seem obviously true and in little need of defense. After all, they will say, the contemporary mind-body debate is largely about a version of monism (viz., physicalism) and its rivalry with dualism. To other philosophers, the monism-matters thesis will seem obviously false—and perhaps even quaint. In spite of the historical connection to monism, they will say, the contemporary debate has a life of its own and should not be tethered to its origins. But on reflection, both of those positions are questionable. As I hope to show, whether monism matters is a complex issue, with arguments worth considering on both sides.[1]

2. Chapter summaries

I will begin Chapter 1 by explaining what I take the relevant monist doctrine to be. I will also describe examples of monist theories, non-monist theories, and theories that might be either monist or non-monist. Then I will explain

[1] For a list of those arguments, see Chapter 9, Section 1.

Monism Matters. Torin Alter, Oxford University Press.
DOI: 10.1093/9780198931560.003.0001

the monism-matters thesis, note some considerations in its favor, and place it in historical context.

In Chapter 2, I will consider three arguments against the monism-matters thesis. The first two emphasize the idea that how the concrete world is divided into types (that is, how relevant types are individuated) is an arbitrary matter. In response, I will argue that how *fundamental* types are individuated is not arbitrary—at least not in a way that threatens the monism-matters thesis. The third argument emphasizes the idea that, when it comes to ontology, philosophers should defer to physics, which is neutral with respect to monism's truth or falsity. In response, I will argue that the extent to which such a deferential attitude is warranted is limited: more so than would be required to undermine the monism-matters thesis.

In Chapter 3, I will present two arguments for the monism-matters thesis. One is that considerations about monism matter because of their relevance to how the main traditional theories in the philosophy of mind—physicalism, dualism, idealism, and neutral monism—are formulated and which of those theories, if any, is true. The other argument is that considerations about monism matter because they help explain why physicalism, idealism, and neutral monism entail supervenience theses, such as the physicalist thesis that mental phenomena supervene on fundamental physical phenomena.

In Chapter 4, I will defend the second of those arguments against four objections. One is that monist theories entail supervenience theses not because of monism but rather because of how we choose to define those theories. In response, I will argue that monism helps explain why we define those theories in that way. The second objection is that, at least in the case of physicalism, there is nothing to explain: contrary to received wisdom, physicalism does not entail that mental phenomena supervene on fundamental physical phenomena (Montero 2013, Montero and Brown 2018, Zhong 2021, Moorfoot 2024). In response, I will argue that the objection is based on dubious reasoning, which runs afoul of physicalism's monist commitments. The third and fourth objections are based on arguments that challenge another received view to which I will appeal: the view that metaphysical grounding entails supervenience (Leuenberger 2014, Skiles 2015). In response, I will argue that both of those objections derive from misunderstandings about the content of the relevant supervenience theses.

In Chapter 5, I will present a third argument for the monism-matters thesis: considerations about monism help explain why physicalism, idealism, and neutral monism entail what I will call *repudiation theses*, such as the physicalist's repudiation of fundamental mentality. Then I will consider a challenge to the latter repudiation thesis (Dorsey 2011, Zhong 2016, Brown 2021, 2023). I will argue that the challenge can be answered by clarifying the relevant sense of "fundamental mentality."

In Chapter 6, I will present three more arguments for the monism-matters thesis, all of which concern how to define the physical for the purposes of the mind-body debate. The first argument concerns whether the physical can be defined negatively, as the not-fundamentally-mental. The second argument concerns whether the physical can be defined deferentially, in terms of what physics posits. The third argument concerns whether the dispute about physicalism's compatibility with fundamental mentality is merely verbal. I will argue that considerations about monism (along with other considerations) imply both that the physical should be defined neither negatively nor deferentially and that the dispute about physicalism's compatibility with fundamental mentality is not merely verbal. Further, I will argue, each of these implications constitutes a reason to accept the monism-matters thesis.

In Chapters 7 and 8, I will zoom in on the question of how best to define the physicalist version of monism.[2] In Chapter 7, I will consider whether physicalism can be defined in terms of supervenience. Terence Horgan (1993), Andrew Melnyk (2003, ch. 2), Jessica M. Wilson (2005, 2021), and others argue that it cannot. Robert J. Howell (2009, 2013) criticizes their arguments, and I will defend his criticism against objections by Wilson (2021). However, I will argue that it can be circumvented by modifying one of their arguments.

In Chapter 8, I will propose a definition of physicalism on which all actual, concrete phenomena are or are ultimately grounded in only primitively physical phenomena. Then I will propose a way to define what it means for something to be physical. I will do that by amending Howell's (2013) neo-Cartesian definition of a physical property, according to which physical properties are fully characterizable in terms of their spatiotemporal implications. The amended definition allows for the possibility that the properties captured by Howell's definition are underlain by even more basic phenomena. The latter would be the case if, for example, spacetime turns out to be derivative. The amended definition also adds a necessary condition: all physical phenomena are structural, in a certain neo-Carnapian sense.

[2] I focus on physicalism because of its centrality to the contemporary mind-body debate. Here I take no stand on whether that (or any) version of monism is true. Elsewhere (Alter 2023) I argue against standard versions of physicalism.

I will begin Chapter 9 with a brief recap of the arguments from Chapters 2 through 6 for and against the monism-matters thesis. Then I will discuss another potential implication of physicalism's monist commitments. Those commitments, I will argue, complicate attempts to reconcile physicalism with moral realism. If sound, that argument indicates yet another way in which monism is philosophically significant.

1
Monism and the Mind-Body Debate

I will begin this chapter with a discussion of monism and its role in the mind-body debate. Then I will explain the monism-matters thesis, note some considerations in its favor, and place it in historical context.

1. Type monism

According to monism, there is fundamentally only one type of phenomenon. In other words, everything shares the same fundamental nature. The most prominent versions of monism are physicalism, idealism, and neutral monism. These theories differ according to how they characterize the nature that they take everything to share. That shared nature is physical according to physicalism, mental according to idealism, and neutral according to neutral monism, where neutral phenomena are neither physical phenomena nor mental phenomena but underlie both.[1]

Monism contrasts with pluralism, according to which there is more than one fundamental type of phenomenon, and with nihilism, according to which there are no such fundamental types. The most prominent version of pluralism is mind–body dualism, which posits two fundamental, ontologically distinct types: the mental and the physical.[2] A potential example of nihilism is a view associated with W. v. o. Quine (1960), on which the very idea of a fundamental type is rejected as baseless or incoherent.

Though somewhat vague, the preceding description of monism and its rivals will suffice for most of what I will say in this book. Nevertheless, it will be instructive to formulate the main monist thesis a bit more precisely, in a

[1] According to some versions of neutral monism, neutral properties can be identical to either physical or mental properties (James 1890, Mach 1910). But even on those versions, neutral properties are neither intrinsically mental nor intrinsically physical (Wishon 2021, Stubenberg and Wishon 2023). In any case, here I set those versions aside.

[2] Unless otherwise specified, by "dualism" I mean mind–body dualism.

Monism Matters. Torin Alter, Oxford University Press. © Torin Alter 2026.
DOI: 10.1093/9780198931560.003.0002

way geared toward the question of monism's significance for the contemporary mind-body debate. I propose the following formulation:

> *Main monist thesis (MT).* All actual, concrete phenomena are such that there is exactly one unified, substantive, fundamental nature that they share.[3]

Let me explain.[4]

Phenomena. I use "phenomena" broadly, to refer to entities, objects, properties, relations, events, stuffs, etc., and parts thereof. "Phenomena" is sometimes used more narrowly. For example, in the Kantian tradition, it refers only to experiential entities ("appearances"). But as I use the term, there is no such restriction on its reference class.

Actual. The "actual" restriction on MT's scope excludes phenomena that do not exist but might have existed. I include this restriction because our topic is monism's role in the mind-body debate, and actual phenomena are that debate's primary concern. Such phenomena are not the debate's sole concern. Indeed, mind–body issues often turn on the modal status of non-actual phenomena such as philosophical zombies—consciousness-free creatures that are physically and functionally identical to ordinary, conscious human beings (Chalmers 1996). But in this context, zombies and their non-actual ilk are discussed primarily for the purpose of addressing issues about actual phenomena, such as how consciousness relates to the rest of nature (Stoljar 2022).[5]

Concrete. Similar points apply to the "concrete" restriction, which excludes abstract phenomena, such as numbers, Platonic forms, etc., from MT's scope. I include this restriction because concrete phenomena are the mind-body debate's primary concern (Schaffer 2017, pp. 14–15; Witmer 2017; *pace* Schneider 2017).[6]

[3] If no actual, concrete phenomena exist, then MT comes out as vacuously true. If that result is undesirable, then we could conjoin MT with "Some actual, concrete phenomena exist."

[4] I sometimes omit qualifications that MT includes. For example, instead of "unified, substantive, fundamental nature," I sometimes use "nature." Another example: instead of "all actual, concrete phenomena," I sometimes use "all phenomena" or "everything."

[5] See Chapter 3, Section 1 and Chapter 4, Section 4.

[6] I do not claim that issues concerning abstract phenomena are irrelevant the mind-body debate. I claim only that such issues are not the debate's primary concern. There are other issues in the vicinity that I ignore for similar reasons. For example, I ignore issues concerning how a monist view such as physicalism could account for the truth that everything is self-identical or for the holes in Swiss cheese (Pautz, forthcoming).

There is exactly one. As Jonathan Schaffer (2018, sec 1.1) observes, any monist theory "attributes oneness" to something, relative to a certain way of counting. That to which oneness is attributed is the *target*, and the way of counting is the *unit*. In MT, the target is all actual, concrete phenomena, and the unit is fundamental type, kind, category, or nature (I use those terms interchangeably). Because of the unit, this sort of monism is known as *type monism*. Type monism has no clear implications for other widely discussed versions of monism. For example, type monism does not entail token monism, according to which there is only one object (Horgan and Potrč 2000, Cornell 2016) or only one substance (Spinoza 1677/2018). Nor does type monism entail priority monism, according to which "the world has parts, but the parts are dependent fragments of an integrated whole" (Schaffer 2010, p. 33). Unless otherwise specified, by "monism" I mean type monism.

Monism of the sort that concerns us here is a metaphysical doctrine, not an epistemic one, and MT reflects that fact. MT does not entail that we know, or even can know, much about the shared nature it posits. This point has special relevance for physicalism, which is sometimes described in partly epistemic terms (e.g., Dupré 1988). Here I assume that physicalism does not have any essential epistemic components. But even if it does, this is not due to physicalism's being a version of monism.

Shared fundamental nature. To say that *x* and *y share* a fundamental nature is to say that *x*'s fundamental nature and *y*'s fundamental nature are one and the same. What does "fundamental nature" mean here? The general idea could be put roughly as follows.[7] For all *x*, *x*'s fundamental nature *FN* is the type of phenomenon *x* fundamentally is. More precisely, *FN* is the type of phenomenon *x* is at an especially fundamental level of analysis: the level that corresponds to the differences between type monism and its pluralist and nihilist competitors. So, *x*'s fundamental type might be *physical*, *mental*, or *neutral* (or some other fundamental type that is on par with those three, if such there be).

FN is modally essential to *x* in that it is metaphysically impossible for *x* to exist unless *x* has *FN*.[8] But fundamental natures cannot generally be identified with modally essential properties. According to Saul Kripke (1972) and Hilary Putnam (1975), being composed of H_2O molecules is a modally

[7] I mean the remarks that follow only to convey the general idea, not to constitute an adequate definition (they do not). In Chapter 5, Section 4, I will say more about the relevant notion of fundamentality.

[8] Metaphysical possibility is possibility *tout court* (Kripke 1972). See Chapter 3, Section 2.

essential property of water. For example, if they are correct, then there is no possible world with hydrogen-free water. Yet if monism is true, then water's fundamental nature is not its chemical composition. According to monism, water has the same fundamental nature that all other actual, concrete phenomena have, and no other such phenomena share water's chemical composition (except those composed partly of water).

MT is consistent with there being many non-fundamental types of actual, concrete phenomena. For example, water and sand are of different non-fundamental types. But both are of a single fundamental type, if MT is true. Likewise, according to MT, mental phenomena are of the same fundamental type as all other actual, concrete phenomena. That is so whether MT takes the form of physicalism, idealism, or neutral monism.

Unified. The shared nature that MT posits must be unified. It must be a single, non-disjunctive feature. I include this restriction in MT to avoid making the thesis too easy to satisfy. After all, even dualists could grant that every actual, concrete phenomenon is of the disjunctive type, *mental or physical.* There are features that can be expressed disjunctively and could nevertheless qualify as a shared nature. For example, an idealist might say that every actual, concrete phenomenon is either a conscious event, an intentional (or representational) psychological state, or a mind. Yet even for that idealist, there is a deeper unity here. She would count conscious events, intentional psychological states, and minds as all fundamentally mental. Likewise, although a physicalist might say that matter and anti-matter are different kinds of phenomena, he would count matter and anti-matter as both fundamentally physical.[9]

Substantive. The shared nature that MT posits must also be substantive, in the following sense: it must be controversial among physicalists, idealists, neutral monists, and dualists whether that nature is fundamental with respect to actual, concrete phenomena. If such philosophers have no reason to disagree over whether feature *F* is fundamental with respect to actual, concrete phenomena, then *F* is not substantive in the relevant sense.[10] This excludes features such as *being actual, being concrete, existing in time, not being a number* from qualifying. By contrast, *being mental* qualifies as substantive.

[9] I borrow the matter/anti-matter example from Montero 2012. However, she seems to reject the proposition that physicalism entails monism. See ch. 4.2–4.

[10] By "reason to disagree" I mean reason *qua* generic physicalist, *qua* generic idealist, etc. A certain physicalist and a certain idealist might disagree about whether *existing in time* is fundamental with respect to actual, concrete phenomena. But presumably their disagreement would derive from doctrines that go beyond generic versions of physicalism and idealism.

Dualists and idealists take that feature to be fundamental with respect to actual, concrete phenomena, whereas physicalists and neutral monists do not. *Being physical* and *being neutral* also qualify, for parallel reasons.

Not just any philosophical disagreement suffices to satisfy MT's substantiveness constraint. As Schaffer (2018, sec. 1.2) observes, there is philosophical disagreement over features as general as *being*. While Baruch Spinoza (1677/2018 IV pref., II, p. 207) regards *being* "the highest category" of everything in nature, Aristotle (*Meta.* 998b22) does not: "Aristotle is a pluralist about . . . the highest categories, denying that there is any higher category above his *substance*, *quantity*, *quality*, etc." (Schaffer 2018, sec. 1.2). But the existence of that philosophical disagreement does not entail that *being* is substantive in the sense relevant to MT. On the contrary, *being* is not substantive in that sense. Physicalists, idealists, neutral monists, and dualists (in their capacities as generic physicalists, generic idealists, etc.) have no reason to disagree over whether *being* is fundamental with respect to actual, concrete phenomena.

MT does not specify anything about the one nature it posits other than its being unified, substantive, fundamental, and shared by all actual, concrete phenomena. Although specific versions of monism characterize that nature, the main traditional monist theories—physicalism, idealism, and neutral monism—leave some things undetermined. For example, while all idealists agree that everything is fundamentally mental, there is disagreement about what exactly that entails. According to Berkeleyan idealists, all phenomena are either minds, ideas in God's mind, or phenomena grounded entirely in such ideas (Berkeley 1710; cf. Adams 2021). But not all idealist theories are theistic (Pelczar 2015; Yetter-Chappell 2017, 2025; Chalmers 2020b).

There is also disagreement about what it means to be physical, in the sense relevant to physicalism and its rivals. Today, many define the physical deferentially, in terms of what physics posits. But this was not always the case. The *locus classicus* of the non-deferential approach is René Descartes' *Principles of Philosophy*. There he writes, " . . . the nature of matter, or body considered in general, consists . . . simply in its being something which is extended in length, breadth, and depth" (Descartes 1644/1985, p. 244). For over two centuries following the publication of *Principles*, the (or at least *a*) defining feature of the physical was often taken to be three-dimensional spatial extension. More recently, Howell (2012, 2013, ch. 1) has proposed a neo-Cartesian definition of a physical property: "*Neocart:* A property is physical iff it can be fully characterized in terms of the conditions it places on the distribution of things in space over time" (Howell 2013, p. 24; italics in original). Other non-deferential options have also been proposed, such as defining the physical negatively, as the not-fundamentally-mental.[11]

All three of the most prominent monist theories (physicalism, idealism, and neutral monism) seem to entail MT, and MT seems to entail the falsity of pluralism and nihilism, monism's traditional rivals. Those entailments would support my proposal that MT captures the relevant monist thesismonist thesis.

MT is not the only way to characterize that thesis. Schaffer (2018) characterizes it as the thesis that all concrete objects fall under one highest type. He writes,

> . . . let the target t_1 = concrete objects, and let the unit u_1 = highest type. To be a monist for t_1 counted by u_1 is to hold that concrete objects fall under one highest type. The materialist, idealist, and neutral monist are all monists of this sort (*substance monism*). They all agree that concrete objects fall under one highest type, disagreeing only over whether the one highest type is material, mental, or something deeper. (Schaffer 2018, sec. 1.1; italics in original)

Although Schaffer's characterization of monism differs from MT, it is not clear how substantial the differences are. His characterization refers to types, whereas MT refers to natures. But I as noted above, I use those terms interchangeably. His characterization mentions a *highest* type, whereas MT mentions a *fundamental* nature. Yet that difference too seems largely, if not entirely, terminological. His characterization refers to *one* highest type, whereas MT refers to *exactly one* fundamental nature. But the restriction to only one is implied in his characterization ("the one highest type"). His characterization restricts monism's scope to objects, whereas MT's scope includes not only objects but also properties, relations, events, etc. But one might take "objects" to encompass the latter, just as I stipulated that "phenomena" does. MT includes qualifications concerning substantiveness and unity, whereas Schaffer's characterization does not. But arguably, those or equivalent qualifications would have to be added for the same reasons that I include them in MT. For example, presumably Schaffer would not wish to count Cartesian dualism (Descartes 1641/1985, 1644/1985) as a version of type monism simply because Cartesian dualists could allow that all concrete objects fall under the disjunctive type *mental or physical*. If so,

[11] See Chapters 2, 6, and 8.

then his characterization needs something like MT's "unified" qualification. Analogous considerations suggest that his characterization also needs something like MT's "substantive" qualification. In any event, for present purposes, MT will suffice as a relatively precise formulation of the main monist thesismonist thesis.

2. Is type monism necessary or contingent?

MT is a contingent thesis about the actual world. It says that all actual, concrete phenomena share a single, unified, substantive fundamental nature. MT is silent on how many such natures there might have been. So, for example, the physicalist version of MT—that is, MT conjoined with the specification of shared nature it posits as *physical*—is compatible with the existence of a possible world in which mind–body dualism is true. This feature of MT reflects the dominant view among contemporary physicalists and their opponents that physicalism is a contingent thesis about actual phenomena rather than a necessary thesis about all possible phenomena (Smart 1959, Putnam 1967, Armstrong 1968; Lewis 1966, 1980, 1986; Chalmers 1996, Stoljar 2022). Plausibly, the same is true of the other versions of monism, such as idealism, and of monism's competitors, such as dualism: they are contingent theses (in the same sense).

Here two remarks are in order. First, to say that physicalism is a contingent thesis is not to say that it lacks modal implications, that is, implications for non-actual possible worlds. On the contrary, physicalism entails the modal thesis that the mental supervenes on the physical. A similar point applies to MT: though about actual phenomena, MT has modal implications.[12] Second, although MT is a contingent thesis, certain monists take their theory to be necessarily true. George Berkeley might be an example. In arguing for idealism, he writes: "the very notion of what is called matter or corporeal substance, involves a contradiction in it" (Berkeley 1710, sec. 9).[13] He appears to derive the contradiction from the assumption that matter and corporeal substance are mind independent by definition. Thus, presumably he would

[12] Arguably, those implications derive from the fact that monism concerns the fundamental nature of actual phenomena. See and 4.

[13] Anti-physicalist arguments such as The Conceivability Argument (Chalmers 1996) would seem to entail a related conclusion that there is no possible world in which physicalism is true and yet consciousness exists, that is, that in all possible worlds, either physicalism is false or consciousness does not exist. See Chapter 3, Section 1.

argue that neither physicalism nor dualism could have been true, that is, that there is no metaphysically possible world that either of those theories accurately describes (Segal and Goldschmidt 2017, p. 35).[14] But merely accepting monism, including idealist monism, does not commit one to anything more than a contingent thesis, albeit one with modal implications.

Crane (2000) disagrees. In his view, monism and dualism should both be understood as necessary theses, that is, theses that are necessarily true if actually true. Otherwise, he suggests, "materialist monism" would entail dualism. In reference to materialist monism, he writes,

> . . . if it were contingent, then there are worlds in which disembodied minds exist, and therefore mind and body are (in some sense) capable of separate existence. But this is what is definitive of dualism.

Call the thesis that "mind and body are (in some sense) capable of separate existence" *The Separability Thesis*. Is The Separability Thesis "definitive of dualism," as Crane suggests?

That does not appear to be the case. As I indicated above, many who reject dualism, including many physicalists, accept The Separability Thesis. Further, denying it would saddle physicalism with what appears to be an unnecessary burden. Physicalists maintain that, as a matter of fact, there are no such things as non-physical ghosts (supernatural creatures with minds, who fly through walls, have magical powers, etc.). But to deny The Separability Thesis is, in effect, to maintain the much stronger claim that there is no possible world in which such things exist. On the face of it, one could be a physicalist without maintaining the latter, stronger claim, just as one could be an idealist without embracing Berkeley's strong claim that the existence of mind-independent phenomena is impossible. Such strong claims might be justified. But justifying them would require more than accepting a version of monism, such as physicalism or idealism. It would require providing a further argument, such as Berkeley's argument that "the very notion of what is called matter or corporeal substance, involves a contradiction in it." Denying The Separability Thesis also seems hard to reconcile with the doctrine that mental states are multiply realizable—a doctrine to which physicalists often

[14] Not all versions of physicalism and dualism posit matter or corporeal substance. But all familiar versions posit mind-independent phenomena of some sort. That might be enough to make them targets of Berkeley's argument. See Rickless (2013, ch. 3) and Downing (2021, sec. 2).

subscribe (Putnam 1967, Lewis 1980, Pereboom 2002, 2011). Putnam (1967) suggests that, in principle, mental states could have been realized by non-physical phenomena even if, in fact, physicalism is true.

Aaron Segal and Tyron Goldschmidt (2017) argue idealism is not merely a contingent thesis: "if idealism is true, then necessarily, everything is purely mental" (p. 36). They also contend that a parallel claim is true of physicalism—that it too is "necessarily true if true at all" (p. 38). However, they use the terms "idealism" and "physicalism" for theories "about what possible features there are—not just about what features are *instantiated* but about what features are *available to be instantiated*" (p. 38; italics in original). That is unusual. Those terms are usually used for theories about actual objects and features that are actually instantiated, not features that are merely available to be instantiated (again recall the view of Lewis et al. that physicalism is compatible with the existence of possible worlds containing non-physical phenomena). Segal and Goldschmidt are free to use "idealism" and "physicalism" in a novel way. But doing so makes the implications of their argument for the mainstream theories in the contemporary mind-body debate unclear.

3. Hard cases

Physicalism, idealism, and neutral monism are versions of monism, whereas mind–body dualism is not. But there are related theories that are hard to classify as monist or non-monist. In this section, I will describe a few examples.

One is Russellian monism, despite being so-called (Chalmers 1997, 2013; Alter and Pereboom 2023a).[15] This theory is often described partly in terms of a distinction between structural and non-structural properties. Regarding structural properties, David J. Chalmers writes:

> . . . a structural property is one that can be fully characterized using structural concepts alone, which I take to include logical, mathematical, and nomic concepts, perhaps along with spatiotemporal concepts. . . (Chalmers 2013, p. 256).

[15] I understand "Russellian monism" to be Millian name, not a description (Mill 1843, vol. 1, bk. I; Kripke 1972, lec. 2). On this understanding, Russellian monism need not be a version of monism any more than a Guinea pig need be a version of a pig.

Potential examples include paradigmatic physical properties, such as *mass, charge, being a subatomic particle,* and *orbiting an atom's nucleus* (Chalmers 1996, p. 153, 2010, pp. 120–21).[16] By contrast, a non-structural property is one that cannot be fully characterized using only structural concepts. According to Russellian monism, there are both structural properties and *quiddities*: non-structural properties that both underlie structural, physical properties and help constitute consciousness.[17]

Is Russellian monism a version of monism? This is not clear. On the one hand, structural properties and quiddities are often presented as different types of property—types that do not share an underlying fundamental nature. One might therefore argue that Russellian monism is a version of dualism. It is not the dualism of Descartes (1641/1985, 1644/1985), according to which the mental and the physical reside in different realms. According to Russellian monism, there is only one realm, in which mental and physical phenomena are intertwined. Even so, if there is an ontological distinction between structural properties and quiddities, and there is no single, underlying fundamental nature that unifies them, then the resulting theory would appear to be dualistic.

On the other hand, Russellian monists might hold that there is ultimately only one sort of fundamental property, which exists in various conditions—conditions that are not themselves instantiations of an ontologically distinct sort of fundamental property. That one sort of property is quiddistic. On this interpretation, structural features do not enjoy an independent ontological status. Physical terms such as "mass" and "charge" refer not to the structural features that physical descriptions express explicitly but instead to underlying non-structural quiddities (Chalmers 1996, p. 155). Thus, Russellian monism might come out as a version of monism after all.[18]

Russellian monism is not the only theory that could be understood either as monism or as dualism. Another such theory is Aristotelian hylomorphism,

[16] See Chapter 8, Section 5. Chalmers (2010, 2020a) suggests that all physical properties are structural. But this is controversial. See Stoljar (2015, 2020a), Alter (2016), and Alter and Pereboom (2023b).

[17] Russellian quiddities differ from Lewisian quiddities, which bear no special relation to consciousness (Lewis 1990). See ch. 8.4–5. How to understand the nature of Russellian quiddities is controversial. See, for example, Pereboom (2011, ch. 5) and Coleman (2015).

[18] Monist Russellian monism could be a version of physicalism, idealism, or neutral monism, depending on how quiddities are construed (Alter and Nagasawa 2012, Alter and Pereboom 2023a). Construing them as physical properties results in Russellian physicalism (Montero 2015, Brown 2017b). Construing them as mental properties results in Russellian idealism (Chalmers 2020b). Construing them as neutral properties results in Russellian neutral monism (Chalmers 1996, p. 155).

on which the mind is taken to be the form of the body (Aristotle, *De Anima* ii 1, Jaworski 2016). This theory too invokes a distinction between two sorts of phenomena: form and matter. Whether the theory is monist or dualist depends on how that distinction is understood. If form and matter are ontologically distinct fundamental property types, which are not underlain by an even more fundamental unifying feature, then the theory is a version of dualism. But if, for example, form ultimately consists in matter, then the theory might be a version of monism. Parallel reasoning applies *mutatis mutandis* to dual-aspect theory (Feigl 1958), which relies on a distinction between mental aspects and physical aspects.

Another example is Immanuel Kant's (1781/87) transcendental idealism. Kant posits two sorts of entities: transcendentally ideal things-in-themselves or *noumena*, and empirically real appearances or *phenomena*. But there is disagreement among Kant scholars about how, according to Kant's theory, noumena and phenomena relate to each other (van Cleve 1999, pp. 6–8). There is a monist interpretation on which fundamentally there are only noumena. There is also a dualist interpretation on which phenomena (that is, appearances) have their own fundamental nature, which is distinct from that of noumena—and on which there is no underlying fundamental nature shared by both.

Yet another hard case is anatta, the Buddhist no-self view (*The Milinda Pañha*). Here again the theory could be understood in different ways, and only some understandings are consistent with monism. Part of the point of denying that selves exist is to reject the assumption that there is a fundamental difference between one's self and the rest of the concrete world. That much is consistent with monism. Perhaps everything, including selves, shares a single fundamental nature. But anatta could be understood as rejecting the very idea of a fundamental nature as baseless or incoherent (Garfield 2015). On that nihilist understanding, the theory is not consistent with monism.

4. The monism-matters thesis

Thus far I have been discussing what the relevant sort of monism is. I now turn to its significance. Here again is this book's main thesis:

> *Monism matters.* Considerations about monism figure importantly in the contemporary mind-body debate.

Let me explain.

Considerations about monism. I use the phrase "considerations about monism" to refer to considerations that concern monism and its non-monist rivals. For example, the fact that idealism is not a version of dualism is no less a consideration about monism than is the fact that idealism is a version of monism.

The contemporary mind-body debate. I use the phrase "the contemporary mind-body debate" to refer to a philosophical debate in the analytic tradition about the relationship between the mental and the physical (Alter and Howell 2012, Chalmers 2021). That debate is "contemporary" in that it is taking place today and has been on-going for at least seventy-five years. It concerns issues such as these: Is the mind the brain? How does a physical system such as a brain generate consciousness? Is consciousness physical? Does it even exist? Is intentionality physical? Does the persistence of a person depend on the persistence of their body? According to the monism-matters thesis, considerations about monism figure importantly in the contemporary philosophical debate concerning at least some such issues. The thesis is neutral on whether monism matters to other debates, including parallel debates in other (e.g., continental and non-Western) traditions.

Figure importantly. By saying that considerations about monism *figure importantly* in the contemporary mind-body debate, I mean that such considerations play a significant philosophical role in that debate. That claim is meant to be incompatible with such considerations playing no philosophical role or only a negligible philosophical role. The claim is also meant to be incompatible with such considerations playing only a non-philosophical role, for example, a psychological role. In other words, the monism-matters thesis says that the contemporary mind-body debate cannot proceed without substantial loss in philosophical content independently of considerations about monism. That does not imply that monism's role is always made explicit. On the contrary, in my view, considerations about monism do not always receive the attention they deserve.

Consider the following two facts. *Fact 1:* split-brain patients appear to exhibit disunified consciousness under certain laboratory conditions. *Fact 2:* a medical purpose of severing the corpus collosum is to treat people with severe epilepsy. Fact 1 figures importantly in the contemporary mind-body debate: it plays a significant philosophical role in the literature on personal identity and the unity of consciousness. For example, Derek Parfit (1984, ch. 12) invokes Fact 1 in arguing for Reductionist view about personal identity over time.[19] He mentions Fact 2 (Parfit 1984, p. 245), but it is incidental to his argument. Fact 2 probably does not figure importantly in any part of the contemporary mind-body debate (as far as I know, it does not). The monism-matters thesis implies that, with respect to figuring in the contemporary mind-body debate, considerations about monism are like Fact 1 and (probably) unlike Fact 2.

The monism-matters thesis does not entail that monism is true. Nor does the thesis entail that monism bears significantly on every aspect of the mind-body debate. It does not. To illustrate, suppose MT is false: there is no one substantive, unified, fundamental nature shared by all actual, concrete phenomena. One might still ask whether, for example, consciousness supervenes on a combination of the various and sundry types of physical phenomena. That question, which bears on physicalism's truth or falsity, can be addressed independently of considerations about monism, at least to a significant extent. Discussion of that issue does not typically involve much that appears to turn on considerations about monism.[20] Why, then, should one accept the monism-matters thesis?

I will provide several reasons. I will state them briefly now and elaborate in Chapters 3 through 6. One reason is that considerations about monism figure importantly in two significant parts of the contemporary mind-body debate: (i) the part that concerns how to formulate the main traditional theories and (ii) the part that concerns which of those theories, if any, is true. Regarding (i), traditionally, physicalism, idealism, and neutral monism are taken to contrast with dualism partly in that they are versions of monism whereas dualism is not. Regarding (ii), considerations about monism bear importantly on significant arguments for and against those theories. For example, one such argument emphasizes that in the rivalry between physicalism and dualism, physicalism has the advantage of parsimony. Arguably, physicalism has that advantage precisely because of considerations about monism: physicalism posits one fundamental nature where dualism posits two.

Another reason to accept the monism-matters thesis is that some core commitments of physicalism, idealism, and neutral monism can be explained partly by the fact that each is a version of monism. Specifically, that fact helps explain why those theories are committed to supervenience theses,

[19] According to Parfit's (1984, p. 210; italics in original) Reductionist view, "the fact of a person's identity over time just consists in the holding of certain more particular facts, and . . . [t]hese facts can be described in an *impersonal* way."

[20] See, for example, Chalmers (1996, Part II) and Howell (2013).

such as the physicalist's thesis that mental phenomena supervene on fundamental physical phenomena (Chapters 3 and 4), and to a repudiation thesis, such as the physicalist's repudiation of fundamental mentality (Chapter 5). Finally, considerations about monism help in addressing other significant mind–body issues, such as how to define the physical for the purposes of formulating physicalism and its competitors (Chapter. 6). For example, the idea that physicalism is a version of monism helps explain why the physical must be defined in a unified way—a result that creates a problem for defining the physical either deferentially, by reference to what physical theory posits, or negatively, as the not-fundamentally-mental.

5. Monism's rise and fall

In the contemporary mind–body literature, monism is not often discussed—at least not as often as one might expect if the monism-matters thesis is true. In this section, I will suggest reasons why this might be.

I will begin by providing some historical context. The contemporary mind-body debate derives from debates in which monism figures prominently. Consider what is perhaps the earliest known expression of a philosophical doctrine in Western philosophy: all is water. That doctrine, which Aristotle (*Meta.* 983b27-33) attributes to Thales of Miletus, could be interpreted as a version of monism in the sense of MT. On that version, the fundamental nature that everything shares is, to borrow a term from David Braddon-Mitchell (2003), *aqueous*. Aqueous monism has turned out to be false: water is composed of more basic phenomena (it is H_2O). Nevertheless. aqueous monism could be seen as a model for subsequent ontological theories. Several ancient Greek philosophers sought a single *arché* underlying the vastly diverse phenomena found in nature.[21] For example, consider the view associated with Leucippus and Democritus, that all is atoms and void (Berryman 2022, sec. 2). This view might qualify as monism if atoms and void are of the same fundamental type, or as dualism if they are of different fundamental types.

The mind-body debate can be seen as a continuation of that pre-Socratic discussion. The apparent difference between mental phenomena and physical phenomena poses a distinctive challenge to the monist ideal, and this

[21] The term "*arché*" is sometimes translated as "first principle" (Guthrie 1962, p. 7), which I take to be more or less equivalent to what I mean by "fundamental nature."

has been recognized for centuries if not millennia. In that sense, historically the mind–body problem has long been at least partly about monism and its rivals. Moreover, the contemporary mind-body debate traces directly to the ontological debate between Cartesian dualists and their monist opponents.

In subsequent mind-body debates, attention to ontological issues about monism and dualism persisted. For example, such issues are front and center in C. D. Broad's authoritative study from 1925, *The Mind and Its Place in Nature*. Broad bases his taxonomy of theories—the "*seventeen* different types of metaphysical theory" that he thinks "are possible theoretically on the relation between Mind and Matter" (Broad 1925, p. 607; italics in original)—partly on the distinction between monism and pluralism. The section entitled "The Seventeen Types of Theory" begins with this statement: "In order to understand the discussion that follows the reader should refer back to the section on Pluralism and Monism in Chapter I . . . " (p. 607). By contrast, in contemporary discussions of the mind–body problem, monism and pluralism are rarely mentioned, let alone discussed in detail. What happened?

One likely factor is that nowadays much of the debate focuses on only two theories: physicalism and dualism. Given that relatively narrow focus, it is perhaps not surprising that the broader categories of monism and pluralism are emphasized less than they were in and prior to Broad's day. And that proposition is consistent with the truth of the monism-matters thesis.

Another likely factor is with a point I noted in Section 4: some widely discussed mind–body issues can be addressed independently of considerations about monism, at least to a significant extent. I mentioned one example: whether consciousness supervenes on physical phenomena of various kinds. There are others as well, for example, whether all truths about consciousness can be a priori deduced from the complete physical truth (Jackson 1982, Chalmers 1996). Much of the debate about those issues does not appear to turn on considerations about monism. But even if some issues in the contemporary mind-body debate are independent of such considerations, arguably others are not.

Those two factors—the narrow focus on physicalism and dualism, and the fact that important mind–body issues seem substantially independent of monism—help explain why attention to monism in the mind–body literature has decreased. But I do not think that is the whole explanation. A third likely factor is a shift in how mind–body issues are seen: a shift that traces to logical positivism. Let me explain.

At least some logical positivists were physicalists. Indeed, according to Rudolf Carnap (1955, p. 312), the term "physicalism" was coined by positivist

Otto Neurath (1931, p. 54). But positivists rejected the traditional way the mind–body problem was understood. According to their verification theory of meaning, statements that cannot be empirically (dis)confirmed, and which are neither analytically true nor analytically false, are meaningless (Creath 2023).[22] Traditionally, the mind–body problem was formulated in metaphysical terms, resulting in theories that neither admit of empirical (dis)confirmation nor are analytically true or analytically false. The positivists therefore saw the traditional mind–body problem as a pseudo-problem. In their view, the real mind–body problem concerns semantic/epistemic issues, such as whether psychology, biology, and chemistry can be reduced to physics. Such a reduction might require semantic principles connecting the vocabulary of psychology, biology, and chemistry to that of physics in ways that can be empirically verified (Neurath 1931, Stoljar 2022, 1.1). Thus, under positivism, physicalism looked somewhat different than it does today. Crane describes the situation as follows:

> The positivists did not see physicalism as an ontological doctrine, since traditional ontological questions were either meaningless ("is there one substance or two?") or transformed into scientific questions ("is matter corpuscular?"). Their concerns were epistemological or methodological: when organising the data of experience, should we adopt the language of physics or a phenomenalistic language of sense-data? To affirm physicalism is to hold that the language of physics is the language we should adopt in giving an account of the world. (Crane 2000, p. 76)

Positivism is now a relic of history. The mind-body debate has refocused on traditional metaphysical questions about the relationship between the mental and the physical, and the discussion is no longer constrained by verificationism. But when it comes to certain questions, positivism's influence is not hard to discern. Consider the question of what counts as physical. Currently, the dominant tendency is to take a deferential, hands-off approach: the nature of the physical should be determined by science, not philosophy. "Physical" entities are those posited by physics. More generally, as Crane writes,

[22] A sentence is analytically true if and only if it is true in virtue of the meanings of the component words. To use a hackneyed example, "No bachelors are married" is analytically true, and "Some bachelors are married" is analytically false.

> Contemporary physicalism comes in many forms, but in its central forms, it retains the positivist view about the priority of physics. This view is transformed, in post-positivist philosophy, into an ontological doctrine: physical science sets the ontological standards and tells us whether a given entity meets these standards. (Crane 2000, p. 76)

Given the positivist-influenced tendency to defer to science when it comes to ontology, it is no wonder that a metaphysical doctrine such as monism—which is associated with a traditional, largely a priori approach to ontology—would be relegated to the periphery of the mind-body debate.[23] Or rather, it is no wonder that some are reluctant to refer expressly to considerations about monism, even where such considerations are relevant.

6. Conclusion

I began this chapter by describing monism and its rivals. I initially characterized monism as the view that there is fundamentally only one type of phenomenon. I then proposed that type monism can be formulated more precisely as MT: the thesis that all actual, concrete phenomena are such that there is exactly one unified, substantive, fundamental nature that they share. I argued that monism should be understood as a contingent thesis, rather than a necessary one—a conclusion that MT reflects. And I gave examples of monist theories (physicalism, idealism, and neutral monism), non-monist theories (dualism and nihilism), and theories that could be either monist or non-monist, depending on how they are explicated (Russellian monism, hylomorphism, dual-aspect theory, transcendental idealism, and anatta).

Next, I turned to the monism-matters thesis: the thesis that considerations about monism figure importantly in the contemporary mind-body debate. I explained what this means: that considerations about monism and its non-monist rivals play a significant philosophical role in the contemporary mind-body debate, that is, in the debate in contemporary analytic philosophy concerning the relationship between the mental and the physical—a debate that has been ongoing for at least seventy-five years. I also briefly

[23] Even when cast in positivist terms, physicalism might entail monism in some sense, though not in the sense of MT. Neurath (1931, p. 54; italics in original) writes, "For 'physicalism' it is essential that *one* kind of *order* is the foundation of all laws, whichever science is concerned, geology, chemistry or sociology."

described some reasons for accepting the monism-matters thesis. I said that considerations about monism help in (i) motivating physicalism, idealism, and neutral monism; (ii) explaining core commitments of those theories, such as their commitments to supervenience and repudiation theses; and (iii) addressing other mind–body issues, such as how to define the physical for the purposes of formulating physicalism and rival theories.

Finally, I considered the question of why monism is nowadays discussed less often than one might expect if the monism-matters thesis is true. I identified three likely factors: a tendency to focus on only two theories, physicalism and dualism; the fact that some mainstream issues seem largely independent of considerations about monism; and a positivist-influenced tendency to reject a traditional, a priori approach to ontology with which monism is associated.

2
On Three Arguments Against the Significance of Monism

In this chapter, I will defend the monism-matters thesis from three arguments against it: The Argument from Arbitrariness, The No-Third-Way Argument, and The Argument from Deference.

1. Arbitrariness

The Argument from Arbitrariness and The No-Third-Way Argument each involve a version of the following thought: monism's truth depends on how the concrete world is divided into types, and there are multiple, equally legitimate ways to do that. Barbara Gail Montero illustrates with a simple example:

> How many kinds of things are in my fruit bowl? Is the answer "one," since every item is a fruit? Or should I say "three," since I have apples, oranges, and a grapefruit? . . . It depends on what matters to you. (Montero 2024, p. 240)

Montero's reflections could be seen as suggesting the following argument against the monism-matters thesis. Monism's truth or falsity depends on type individuation, that is, on how the concrete world is divided into types. But type individuation is interest relative and therefore arbitrary. And if monism's truth depends on something arbitrary, then monism is not significant for the mind-body debate: the monism-matters thesis is false. In standard form:

The Argument from Arbitrariness

1. Whether monism is true depends on how types are individuated.
2. How types are individuated is interest relative and therefore arbitrary.

Monism Matters. Torin Alter, Oxford University Press. © Torin Alter 2026.
DOI: 10.1093/9780198931560.003.0003

3. If whether monism is true depends on something arbitrary, then the monism-matters thesis is false.
4. Therefore, the monism-matters thesis is false.

That argument is valid. Is it sound? I think not. Note first that premises 1 and 2 need refining. Monism is a claim about *fundamental* types. So, premises 1 and 2 should be replaced with these:

1.′ Whether monism is true depends on how fundamental types are individuated.
2.′ How fundamental types are individuated is interest relative and therefore arbitrary.

Premise 1′ is plausible. For the sake of argument, I grant premise 3. But why should we accept premise 2′? Montero's fruit-bowl case concerns non-fundamental types (such as *fruit* and *apple*) and so does not establish that premise. Further, how fundamental types are individuated is not clearly interest relative. For example, consider an issue that divides idealists and dualists from physicalists and neutral monists: whether there are fundamentally mental phenomena. That issue does not appear to be interest relative. If there are reasons to conclude otherwise, they are not evident.

Further, even if fundamental-type individuation is interest relative, it does not follow that such individuation is an arbitrary matter. The monism-matters thesis says only that monism matters *for the contemporary mind-body debate*. More specifically, the concern is with what is the most plausible first-order fundamental ontology of actual, concrete phenomena. So, in effect, I have antecedently stipulated which interest is relevant here. Relative to that interest, it does not seem arbitrary how the concrete world is divided into fundamental types.[1]

2. No third way

The Argument from Arbitrariness is one way to understand the argument that the monism-matters thesis runs afoul of arbitrariness in type individuation. Here is another: there are only two non-arbitrary ways to individuate

[1] But see Brown (2026).

fundamental types, and both entail that the monism-matters thesis is false. Let me explain.

One non-arbitrary way to individuate fundamental types is to be highly inclusive and say that *being an actual, concrete phenomenon* is the only fundamental nature shared by all actual, concrete phenomena. But that would make monism trivially true.[2] A second non-arbitrary way to individuate fundamental types is to be highly exclusive. Every actual, concrete phenomenon falls under many types that are more specific than the type *actual, concrete phenomenon*. We might count each of those more specific types as fundamental natures. But then monism would be obviously false. It would be refuted by the fact that *table* and *chair* are distinct types. And, the argument runs, any third way of individuating fundamental types is arbitrary. In standard form:

The No-Third-Way Argument

1. Whether monism is true depends on how fundamental types are individuated.
2. On the highly inclusive way of individuating fundamental types, monism is trivially true.
3. On the highly exclusive way of individuating fundamental types, monism is obviously false.
4. Any third way of individuating fundamental types is arbitrary.
5. If monism is trivially true or obviously false, or if whether it is true depends on something arbitrary, then the monism-matters thesis is false.
6. So, the monism-matters thesis is false.[3]

That argument is valid. Is it sound? I think not. Premises 1, 2, and 3 are plausible. For the sake of argument, I grant premise 5. But premise 4 is

[2] That feature, *being an actual, concrete phenomenon*, is not substantive in the sense MT specifies. See Chapter 1, Section 1.

[3] The No-Third-Way Argument is inspired by a certain reaction to the special composition problem for material objects, that is, the problem of specifying the conditions under which two or more material objects compose a further, composite material object (Hestevold 1981, van Inwagen 1990). Some react by saying that the only plausible answers are compositional universalism (any two material objects compose a further, composite material object) and compositional nihilism (no material objects compose): compositional restrictivism (some collections of material objects compose a further, composite material object, and other collections do not) is ruled out on grounds of arbitrariness (see Cornell 2025).

dubious. Why think that the only non-arbitrary ways of individuating fundamental types are the highly inclusive way and the highly exclusive way? Consider the type *physical.* There is at least a prima facie case for concluding that all actual, concrete phenomena are fundamentally physical. Further, there appears to be no comparable case for concluding that all actual, concrete phenomena are fundamentally chemical, or fundamentally biological, etc. Such categories—the chemical, the biological, etc.—would seem to be more specific forms of the physical. Consider also the type *mental.* There is at least a prima facie case for concluding that at least some actual, concrete phenomena are fundamentally mental. Further, there appears to be no comparable case for concluding that some actual, concrete phenomena are fundamentally intentional, or fundamentally cognitive, etc. Such categories—the intentional, the cognitive, etc.—would seem to be more specific forms of the mental. Thus, the categories of the physical and the mental stand out in what appears to be a non-arbitrary way.

From certain perspectives, there may be nothing special about the categories of the physical and the mental. An example might be the perspective of a philosopher interested only in the aesthetic qualities of a well-executed banana flick in table tennis. But here we are concerned with the perspective of a philosopher interested in the contemporary mind-body debate. Consider an analogy. Relative to an interest in diet and health, the distinction between saturated and unsaturated fats is not arbitrary. Likewise, relative to an interest in the contemporary mind-body debate, the distinction between the physical and the mental is not arbitrary.

3. The Argument from Deference

Another argument against the monism-matters thesis may be stated initially as follows:

The Argument from Deference

1. When it comes to ontology, philosophers should defer to physics.
2. Physics is neutral on whether monism is true.
3. If (i) when it comes to ontology philosophers should defer to physics and (ii) physics is neutral on whether monism is true, then the monism-matters thesis is false.
4. Therefore, the monism-matters thesis is false.

That argument is valid. Is it sound? I think not. But showing why will be slightly complicated. That is because there are at least four ways its premises could be understood, resulting in four versions of the argument. I will evaluate The Argument from Deference indirectly by evaluating each version in turn. Caveat: in formulating those versions, I will not always try to have them mirror the structure of The Argument from Deference. Instead, I will formulate each version in what seems to me the most natural way.

4. The neutrality of physics

Premise 1 of The Argument from Deference might be understood as a claim about how physical phenomena should be defined: they should be defined as phenomena physics posits, whatever those may be. The argument could then be stated as follows:

The Argument from the Neutrality of Physics

1. Physical phenomena are defined as phenomena physics posits.
2. Physics is neutral on whether monism is true.
3. If (i) physical phenomena are defined as phenomena physics posits and (ii) physics is neutral on whether monism is true, then the monism-matters thesis is false.
4. Therefore, the monism-matters thesis is false.

That argument is valid. Is it sound? I think not. The definition that premise 1 asserts faces what is known as Hempel's dilemma (Hempel 1969, 1980; Montero 1999). "Phenomena physics posits" refers to what exists according to physical theory, that is, a theory that articulates the truths of fundamental physics. Which physical theory is relevant? Current physical theory? Presumably not. Current physical theory is incomplete. It might well fail to posit some phenomenon that ought to qualify as physical—perhaps one that would be posited by a future, improved physical theory.[4] How about ideal physical theory? That answer runs into a different problem: we do not know the content of ideal physical theory. In particular, we cannot rule out the possibility that it posits mental phenomena. If so, then physicalists would have

[4] For a defense of defining the physical by reference to current physics, see Melnyk (1997). For a criticism of Melnyk's position, see Montero (1999).

to count such phenomena as fundamental—no less so than, say, quarks.[5] Yet the existence of fundamental mentality is incompatible with (standard) physicalism.[6]

One might respond that the chances of ideal physics positing mental phenomena are remote and therefore of little consequence. But are the chances remote? Not clearly. According to Chalmers and Kelvin J. McQueen (2022), consciousness, a mental phenomenon *par excellence*, might well be what collapses the wave function.[7] Moreover, here the *likelihood* of ideal physics' positing mentality is largely beside the point. Premise 1 ("Physical phenomena are defined as phenomena physics posits") implies an attitude of absolute, unqualified deference to physical theory regarding what counts as physical. That seems misguided, at least for the purposes of physicalism. An adequate basis for demarcating the class of phenomena that physicalists regard as fundamental should ensure that mentality is not included in it, regardless of how unlikely it is that ideal physics would posit mentality.[8]

Let us turn to premise 2: "Physics is neutral on whether monism is true." That premise is not clearly true. Within theoretical physics, there is a longstanding effort to unify the fundamental forces. This seems suggestive of monist aspirations—even if theoretical physicists would be willing to countenance a non-monistic theory, for example, for the sake of completeness.

Finally, consider premise 3: "If (i) physical phenomena are defined as phenomena physics posits and (ii) physics is neutral on whether monism is true, then the monism-matters thesis is false." That premise is dubious. Suppose the antecedent of that conditional (that is, the conjunction of (i) and (ii)) is true. Considerations about monism might nonetheless be significant for the mind-body debate. Indeed, in Chapters 3 through 6, I will argue that monism plays a significant role in explaining core commitments of physicalism, idealism, and neutral monism, such as their commitments to supervenience theses. That would be enough to establish the monism-matters thesis, even given (i) and (ii).

[5] The same problem arises with respect to any unknown future physical theory and for completed physical theory (the latter may or may not be equivalent to ideal physical theory).

[6] Some views described as "physicalist" are compatible with the existence of fundamental mentality (e.g., Strawson 2008). But such views are not standard versions of physicalism (Stoljar 2020b). See Chapter 8, Section 5. Unless otherwise specified, I take "physicalism" to refer only to standard versions.

[7] Cf. Wigner (1962), Goswami (1990), Stapp (1993), and Zhong (2016).

[8] See Chapter 5.

5. No a priori constraints

Premise 1 of The Argument from Deference says, "When it comes to ontology, philosophers should defer to physics." Arguably, that premise is motivated partly by a negative methodological claim: no a priori constraints should be placed on what qualifies as physical. The second version of The Argument from Deference begins with that claim. It is then inferred that physicalism could be true without monism being true, and finally that the monism-matters thesis is false. In standard form:

The Argument from No A Priori Constraints

1. No a priori constraints should be placed on what counts as physical.
2. If no a priori constraints should be placed on what counts as physical, then physicalism could be true without monism being true.
3. If physicalism could be true without monism being true, then the monism-matters thesis is false.
4. So, the monism-matters thesis is false.

That argument is valid. Is it sound? I think not. For the sake of argument, I grant premise 2. But premise 1 is dubious. Why might one accept that premise? Perhaps the best reason concerns the failure of past attempts to define the physical a priori. The Cartesian definition, on which to be physical is to be spatially extended, has turned out to be empirically inadequate. For example, forces such as gravity are physical but not extended, at least not in any obvious sense. Related assumptions about matter—for example, that matter must be "solid, inert, impenetrable and conserved, and to interact deterministically and only on contact" (Crane and Mellor 1990, p. 186)—have fared no better. As Daniel Stoljar writes,

> As the name suggests, materialists historically held that everything was matter—where matter was conceived as "an inert, senseless substance, in which extension, figure, and motion do actually subsist" (Berkeley, *Principles of Human Knowledge*, par. 9). But physics itself has shown that not everything is matter in this sense; for example, forces such as gravity are physical but it is not clear that they are material in the traditional sense . . . (Stoljar 2022, 1.1)[9]

[9] Some take this as a reason to prefer calling the contemporary theory "physicalism" rather than "materialism." But not all do. For example, Lewis (1997, p. 325, fn. 2) writes, "Some fear

Such past failures justify a good dose of caution when considering a priori constraints on the physical.

But that reasonable moral falls short of establishing what premise 1 implies: a prohibition on any a priori constraint whatsoever. To justify such a universal prohibition, more argument would be needed. One might try to address that concern by appealing to an especially strong version of philosophical naturalism: a doctrine that calls for a wholesale rejection of a priori approaches to philosophical issues. But in the present context, that move is dialectically suspicious. Arguably, a proponent of the monism-matters thesis need not accept naturalism of that kind. Moreover, as I noted in Section 4, some a priori constraints on the physical would seem to be called for.[10]

Premise 3 is also questionable. But before discussing it, let me consider a variant of the same argument, which uses that same premise and addresses the concern I just raised about premise 1. This will be our third version of The Argument from Deference.

6. The possible disunity of the physical

Instead of relying on a universal prohibition on constraining the physical a priori, one might begin with a more targeted prohibition: a priori we should not rule out the possibility that ideal physics will posit a fundamentally disunified set of phenomena—phenomena that have little more in common than their all being posited by the same scientific theory. That more targeted prohibition seems reasonable. It is not refuted by arguments I gave in Section 5. And it might seem to create the same problem for the monism-matters thesis that the universal prohibition was supposed to create. Thus, consider:

The Argument from the Possible Disunity of the Physical

1. Ideal physics might posit fundamentally disunified phenomena.
2. If ideal physics might posit fundamentally disunified phenomena, then physicalism could be true without monism being true.

that 'materialism' conveys a commitment that . . . ultimate physics must be a physics of matter alone: no fields, no radiation, no causally active spacetime. Not so! Let us proclaim our solidarity with forebears who, like us, wanted their philosophy to agree with ultimate physics. Let us not chide and disown them for their less advanced ideas about what ultimate physics might say." Another notable example is Chalmers (1996, 2010), who also tends to use "materialism" in reference to the contemporary theory.

[10] See also Chapters 5 and 6.

3. If physicalism could be true without monism being true, then the monism-matters thesis is false.
4. Therefore, the monism-matters thesis is false.

That argument is valid. Is it sound? I think not. For the sake of argument, I grant premise 1. What about premise 2? Physicalism is compatible with the posits of ideal physics not *appearing* to form a fundamentally unified set. But one might argue that those phenomena must in fact be fundamentally unified, or else physicalism is false. Indeed, that conclusion is supported by some of the arguments I will present in Chapters 3 through 6. So, premise 2 is questionable.[11]

Moreover, premise 3—which is also premise 3 of The Argument from No A Priori Constraints—is dubious. Suppose a non-monist version of physicalism could be true. Contrary to premise 3, it does not follow that considerations about monism do not figure importantly in the contemporary mind-body debate. Arguably, they do. For example, arguably they figure importantly in parsimony arguments that favor physicalism over dualism.[12] That is so even if monism is optional for physicalists.

7. Conceptual anachronism

Like The Argument from No A Priori Constraints, a fourth version of The Argument from Deference scrutinizes the concept of the physical and the need to defer to physics to determine that concept's extension. But here the prohibition on a priori constraints plays only a supporting role. The starring role is played by the claim that the concept of the physical is antiquated. In standard form:

The Argument from Conceptual Anachronism

1. If whether monism is true depends on an antiquated concept, then the monism-matters thesis is false.
2. Whether monism is true depends on an antiquated concept, namely, the concept of the physical.
3. Therefore, the monism-matters thesis is false.

[11] See esp. Chapter 5, Section 4.
[12] See Chapter 3, Section 1.

That argument is valid. Is it sound? I think not. Consider premise 1. Suppose monism's truth depends on an antiquated concept. What follows? Perhaps it follows that the contemporary mind-body debate is not philosophically significant insofar as that debate concerns monism. But the monism-matters thesis concerns whether monism is philosophically significant to that debate, not whether that debate is philosophically significant. One might hold that monism matters to a philosophically insignificant debate. So, premise 1 is questionable.

Let us turn to premise 2 ("Whether monism is true depends on an antiquated concept, namely, the concept of the physical"). Why might one accept that premise? Noam Chomsky (1988, 1995) provides a reason. Regarding contemporary discussions of the mind–body problem in analytic philosophy, he writes,

> ... the discussions presuppose some antecedent understanding of what is physical or material, what are the physical entities. These terms had some sense within the mechanical philosophy, but what do they mean in a world based on Newton's "mysterious force," or still more mysterious notions of fields of force, curved space, infinite one-dimensional strings in ten-dimensional space, or whatever science concocts tomorrow? Lacking a concept of "matter" or "body" or "the physical," we have no coherent way to formulate issues related to the "mind–body problem." (Chomsky 1995, pp. 4–5)

Crane and Mellor (1990) argue similarly.[13]

Here we should distinguish two parts of the argument of Chomsky and Crane and Mellor. One is historical. It emphasizes the inadequacy of outdated definitions of the physical, such as Descartes', for grounding a substantive contemporary mind-body debate—definitions that are incompatible with modern (and perhaps even Newtonian) physics. That part of their argument seems unassailable. There is also a non-historical part. In effect, it concludes that the historical problem is irremediable: any attempt to replace outdated definitions of the physical with a new one will also fail. What is their basis for that conclusion?

Chomsky et al. suggest that if we wish to update our conception of the physical, then we can do so only by deferring completely to what science

[13] I will treat Chomsky and Crane and Mellor as giving the same argument. There are differences, but here none matter much.

postulates. For example, regarding the revelations of modern physics about matter, Crane and Mellor write,

> Faced with these discoveries, materialism's modern descendants have—understandably—lost their metaphysical nerve. No longer trying to limit the matter of physics a priori, they now take a more subservient attitude: the empirical world, they claim, contains just what a true complete physical science would say it contains. (Crane and Mellor 1990, p. 186)

Crane and Mellor imply that this "more subservient attitude" is justified. But according to them and to Chomsky, such an attitude cannot deliver an adequate notion of the physical—one that, as Crane and Mellor put it, would fail to make the debate over physicalism's truth or falsity "non-vacuous."

Is the non-historical part of the argument of Chomsky and Crane and Mellor sound? I think not. It would seem to rely on two mistakes I criticized in Sections 4 and 5: inferring from the failures of past a priori definitions of the physical that what counts as physical is not subject to a priori constraints; and replacing the a priori approach to defining the physical with an attitude of absolute, unqualified deference to physics. If my arguments from Sections 4 and 5 are sound, then the latter attitude is problematic and some a priori constraints on the physical are justified. Why, then, should we be so pessimistic about the prospects of devising an adequate definition? In lieu of additional reasons, such pessimism seems unwarranted.

Further, some offer definitions that seem to avoid the sorts of problems Chomsky and Crane and Mellor raise. I will mention three examples. One is Wilson's (2006, 2021) "physics-based NFM account." The "physics-based" part is what I have been calling "deferential": the class of fundamental physical phenomena is determined by the posits of physics. She addresses the concern that such posits might include something mental by adding a "No Fundamental Mentality" (or "NFM") constraint: a stipulation that the class of fundamental physical phenomena shall not include anything fundamentally mental, regardless of what physics posits. Others, including Joseph Levine (2001), define the physical negatively, as the not-fundamentally-mental, resulting in what is known as *via negativa physicalism*. In response to Chomsky, Levine (p. 20) writes, "we don't need a clear conception of the physical to formulate materialism. All we need is a clear, or even not-so-clear, conception of the mental." Still others define the physical positively and non-deferentially, in a way that is sensitive to the concern about repeating past errors. Howell's neocart, on which a property is physical if and only if its nature can be fully characterized by its spatiotemporal implications, is an example.

I do not claim any of those three definitions is fully adequate. On the contrary, in later chapters, I will raise problems for each.[14] My claim is only that they are not refuted by the arguments of Chomsky and Crane and Mellor. I conclude that premise 2 of The Argument from Conceptual Anachronism ("Whether monism is true depends on an antiquated concept, namely, the concept of the physical") has not been established.

8. Conclusion

In this chapter, I defended the monism-matters thesis from three arguments against it. One is The Argument from Arbitrariness, according to which the thesis is false because type individuation is interest relative and therefore arbitrary. In response, I argued that how *fundamental* types are individuated is not arbitrary in a way that threatens the monism-matters thesis. I appealed to similar considerations in response to The No-Third-Way Argument, according to which there is no non-arbitrary way of individuating fundamental types that does not undermine the monism-matters thesis. Then I considered four versions of The Argument from Deference, according to which ontology is determined by the posits of physics, which is neutral on whether monism is true or false. In effect, I argued that all four versions place too much faith in the idea that, when it comes to demarcating the category of the physical, we should defer to physics. Some measure of deference might well be called for. But that is not enough to justify detaching physicalism from monism, let alone concluding that monism plays no significant role in the contemporary mind-body debate.

[14] I will discuss *via negativa* physicalism in Chapter 6, Section 2, the deferential approach in Chapter 6, Section 1, and neocart in Chapter 8, Section 4. In, Chapter 8, Section 5, I will propose a revised version of neocart.

3

Two Arguments for the Significance of Monism

In this chapter, I will present two arguments for the monism-matters thesis: The Motivation Argument and The Argument from Explaining Supervenience.

1. The Motivation Argument

The Motivation Argument is that considerations about monism matter because they figure importantly in two significant parts of the contemporary mind-body debate: the part that concerns how to formulate the main traditional theories and the part that concerns which of those theories, if any, is true. In standard form:

The Motivation Argument

1. Two following two parts of the contemporary mind-body debate are significant: the part that concerns how to formulate the four main traditional theories—physicalism, dualism, idealism, and neutral monism—and the part that concerns which of those theories, if any, is true.
2. Considerations about monism figure importantly into those parts of the debate.
3. If considerations about monism figure importantly into a significant part of the contemporary mind-body debate, then the monism-matters thesis is true.
4. Therefore, the monism-matters thesis is true.

That argument is valid. Is it sound? I think so. Premise 3 is true by definition.[1] Premise 1 is plausible on its face. Since at least the middle of the

[1] See Chapter 1, Section 4.

Monism Matters. Torin Alter, Oxford University Press. © Torin Alter 2026.
DOI: 10.1093/9780198931560.003.0004

seventeenth century, the mind-body debate has focused on dualism, physicalism, and idealism. And although neutral monism did not rise to relative prominence until the early twentieth century, today it is taken seriously (Chalmers 1996, p. 155; Wishon 2021).[2] The issues of how to formulate those four theories and which, if any, is true are both clearly significant to the contemporary mind-body debate. Indeed, the latter issue is about as central to the debate as any.

Premise 2 ("Considerations about monism figure importantly into those parts of the debate") is also plausible for several reasons. Such considerations clearly figure importantly into the part of the debate concerning how to formulate the four main traditional theories: traditionally, physicalism, idealism, and neutral monism are understood to be versions of monism, and mind–body dualism is understood to be a version of pluralism. The traditional approach to theory taxonomy could be rejected. But I am aware of no viable alternative approach that does not also rely on considerations about monism.

I will now describe three ways in which considerations about monism figure importantly in discussions of which, if any, of the four main traditional theories is true.

Way 1: considerations about monism bear importantly on parsimony arguments. Physicalism is often touted as being more parsimonious than dualism: physicalism posits only one fundamental type, whereas dualism posits two. But if detached from monism, physicalism might posit many fundamental types, thereby losing the advantage of parsimony. Similar reasoning applies to idealism and neutral monism, *mutatis mutandis*. Of course, one might value parsimony without endorsing monism. Also, physicalists, idealists, and neutral monists who argue that their theory is superior to dualism on grounds of parsimony might not mention monism explicitly. Nevertheless, familiar parsimony-based arguments for physicalism, et al., would seem to rely on an assumption that, other things being equal, theory *M* is more likely to be true than theory *D* if *D* posits two fundamental types whereas *M* posits only one. And the antecedent of that conditional claim is roughly equivalent to the claim that *M* is a version of monism and *D* is a version of non-monist dualism.

[2] One can find versions of neutral monism in earlier writings, for example, Avenarius (1888/90). The view's origins can be traced to Spinoza (1677/2018) and Hume (1738). See Stubenberg and Wishon (2023, sec. 2).

Way 2: considerations about monism bear importantly on causal arguments. Because dualism posits two fundamental types of phenomena, it quickly runs into the problem of how tokens of those types could interact causally. That fact leads to causal arguments against dualism and for physicalism (Elisabeth 1643; Kim 1989, 1998, chs. 2 and 3; Papineau 2002, ch. 1). Dualists can respond by positing psychophysical bridge laws (Hart 1988; Chalmers 1996, chs. 4 and 6). But such laws can seem ad hoc and thus make the resulting theory inelegant (Smart 1959; Papineau 2002, ch. 1). Plausibly, the relevant causal arguments are aided by the proposition that while physicalism is a version of monism, dualism is not. Here is why. One reason the dualist's psychophysical bridge laws can seem ad hoc is that they are supposed to connect fundamentally disunified phenomena. Arguably, if laws connecting some physical phenomena with other physical phenomena are not similarly problematic, that is partly because of the assumed unity of the physical domain. In other words, it is assumed that the phenomena that physical laws connect are all part of a fundamentally unified system. Monism helps justify that assumption. For example, according to neocart, the nature of any physical property ultimately consists in its spatiotemporal implications. Such fundamental unity among non-fundamentally diverse phenomena helps explain why laws connecting them are not threatened by the sort of principled objections that threaten the dualist's psychophysical laws. Similar reasoning could be used to motivate idealism and neutral monism.[3]

Way 3: considerations about monism bear importantly on anti-physicalist arguments. Consider widely discussed anti-physicalist arguments such as The Conceivability Argument (Chalmers 1996, ch. 4, 2010).[4] The Conceivability Argument is often put in terms of the ideal conceivability of a zombie world: a consciousness-free, minimal physical-and-functional duplicate of the actual world.[5] Ideal conceivability is conceivability on ideal reflection, where a proposition *p* is conceivable on ideal reflection if and only

[3] Berkeley (1710) could be interpreted as employing such reasoning to help motivate idealism. It is less clear that neutral monists do so. But see Mach (1910).

[4] Another such argument is Jackon's (1982, 1995) Knowledge Argument. See Ludlow et al. (2004), Coleman (2019), and Alter (2023). For others, such as the explanatory gap argument (Levine 1983), see Chalmers (1996, pp. 94–106, 2010, pp. 192–205).

[5] Sometimes other cases are used, for example, an inverted world: a minimal physical-and-functional duplicate world where red and green color experiences are inverted (Chalmers 1996, p. 124). Another such case is a comparatively dull world: a minimal physical-and-functional duplicate world where color experiences are slightly duller than they actually are (Stoljar 2006, p. 38).

if no a priori reasoning would reveal any incoherence in *p* (Chalmers 2002).[6] The argument can be stated roughly as follows:

The Conceivability Argument

1. A zombie world is ideally conceivable.
2. If a zombie world is ideally conceivable, then a zombie world is metaphysically possible.
3. If a zombie world is metaphysically possible, then physicalism is false.
4. Therefore, physicalism is false.

There is a sense in which monism is partly what anti-physicalist arguments such as The Conceivability Argument are about. For example, when contemplating whether a zombie world is metaphysically possible, part of what interests us is whether there is a fundamental difference between consciousness and everything else in nature (Chalmers 1996, Parts 1 and 2)—an issue that is roughly equivalent to whether monism is true.

Further, monism is directly relevant to such anti-physicalist arguments. At least some of them concern the alleged modal separability of the mental and the physical, of the sort that the zombie-world scenario illustrates. Why is such modal separability taken to be relevant to physicalism? Part of the answer concerns the monist aspect of physicalism. Consciousness is an actual, concrete phenomenon. So, arguably, if all actual, concrete phenomena—including consciousness—share the same fundamental nature, and that nature is physical, then a minimal physical duplicate of the actual world would have to contain consciousness. Thus, the monist aspect of physicalism helps support The Conceivability Argument's premise 3 ("If a zombie world is metaphysically possible, then physicalism is false").[7] Similar reasoning applies to other anti-physicalist arguments, *mutatis mutandis.*

2. Supervenience theses

That last point, about the connection between physicalism and supervenience, brings us to my third argument for the monism-matters

[6] That biconditional expresses negative (ideal) conceivability (Chalmers 2002). Positive conceivability involves forming a positive conception, such as an image. This distinction does not matter much for present purposes.

[7] I will elaborate in Section 3 and Chapter 4.

thesis: considerations about monism help explain why physicalism, idealism, and neutral monism entail supervenience theses. I will present that argument in the next section. In this section, I will discuss the relevant supervenience theses.

Physicalism entails that the mental supervenes on the physical. That supervenience thesis has been formulated in different ways (Kim 1984, 1993), but Jackson's (1998) formulation is typical:

> *Physicalist supervenience thesis (PSV).* Any world which is a *minimal* physical duplicate of our world is a duplicate *simpliciter* of our world. (Jackson 1998, p. 12; italics in original)[8]

Five remarks are in order. First, PSV's supervenience base—that on which everything else is said to supervene—includes all physical phenomena. But arguably, physicalism is committed to a stronger supervenience thesis, on which the supervenience base includes only *fundamental* physical phenomena. The latter might include only microphysical phenomena, for example (Howell 2013; Chalmers 2004, pp. 286–87, 2010, p. 142; Alter 2023, p. 19).[9] Following Howell (2013, p. 41) I will use "physical*" to refer to fundamental physical phenomena, though I will sometimes omit the asterisk when it is clear from context what I mean. The stronger supervenience thesis can be stated as follows:

> *Physicalist* supervenience thesis (PSV*).* Any world that is a minimal physical* duplicate of our world is a duplicate simpliciter of our world.

To see why PSV* is stronger than PSV, note that PSV is consistent with a possibility that PSV* rules out: the possibility of a world *w* that duplicates all fundamental physical features of the actual world, and contains no further such features, but differs from the actual world with respect to certain non-fundamental features. For example, consider the idea that *w* contains no mushrooms despite being indistinguishable from the actual world with

[8] PSV is not fully precise because it does not address issues arising from indexicality (Chalmers 2010, ch. 6; Alter 2023, ch. 1). But those issues are not especially relevant here. Also, the worlds in the scope of the universal qualifier ("Any world") are *possible* worlds. Analogous points apply to the other supervenience theses I will consider, such as PSV* and ISV*.

[9] I mention microphysical phenomena here only for purposes of illustration. What the most fundamental physical phenomena are is an open question. The question of whether maximally fundamental physical phenomena exist is also open. See Schaffer (2003, 2010).

respect to its fundamental physical features and containing no other fundamental features. PSV* rules out *w* as impossible: *w* is a minimal physical* duplicate of our world but not a duplicate simpliciter of our world. But *w* is not a minimal *physical* duplicate of our world: *w* differs from the actual world with respect to one (non-fundamental) physical feature, namely, the existence of mushrooms. So, PSV does not apply to *w*. Therefore, unlike PSV*, PSV does not rule *w* out as impossible.

Second, let me explain the minimality qualification ("Any world that is a *minimal* physical* duplicate . . . "). Physicalism is a contingent thesis about the actual world.[10] If that thesis is true, then there are no non-physical ghosts. But physicalism is compatible with there being non-actual possible worlds that contain such things, even if those worlds are indistinguishable from the actual world in all physical respects. The "minimal" qualification prevents PSV* from implying otherwise. Due to that qualification, the scope of "Any world" includes only those possible worlds that contain nothing in addition to the same (or exactly similar) physical phenomena that our world contains.[11] PSV* is therefore compatible with the claim that non-minimal duplicate worlds containing non-physical ghosts are possible—a result that comports with the idea that physicalism is a contingent thesis.

Third, the sort of supervenience that PSV* articulates is alethic rather than epistemic. Some versions of physicalism entail epistemic theses. One important such thesis is that, roughly put, all truths about consciousness are a priori entailed by the complete physical truth. Chalmers (1996, 2010) classifies versions of physicalism that entail such an epistemic thesis as "type-A materialism" and versions that do not as "type-B materialism."[12]

Fourth, the sort of alethic necessity that PSV* concerns is metaphysical necessity, that is, necessity *tout court* (Kripke 1972). Metaphysical necessity contrasts with relativized varieties, such as natural necessity, that is, necessity relative to the actual laws of nature (such as the laws of General Relativity) and the actual natural constants (such as the gravitational constant). Cartesian interactionist dualists can accept that the mental naturally supervenes on the physical. But such dualists reject PSV*, which concerns metaphysical necessity (Chalmers 1996, 2010; Rosen 2010).

[10] See Chapter 1, Section 2.

[11] I add "or exactly similar" so as to avoid taking a stand on whether numerically identical objects exist in numerically distinct possible worlds (Kripke 1972, Lewis 1986).

[12] For examples of type-A materialism, see Lewis (1966), Armstrong (1968), Churchland (1996), and Weisberg (2025). For examples of type-B materialism, see Papineau (2002), Block (2006), Balog (2012), and Howell (2013).

Fifth, PSV* is a global supervenience thesis rather than a local one (Kim 1984, 1993). That is, it is a thesis about the entire actual world, rather than a proper part thereof. Some versions of physicalism entail local supervenience theses. For example, according to familiar versions of the (type) identity theory, human mental states supervene on human brain states (Place 1956, Smart 1959, Lewis 1966, Armstrong 1968). Even externalist physicalists, who argue that human mental states supervene partly on features of an individual's physical or social environment (Burge 1979, 1982; Dretske 1995, Ball 2009, Tye 2009), seem committed to a local supervenience thesis. At least, they seem so committed if an individual's "environment" does not comprise the entirety of the world she inhabits.[13] Nevertheless, one could be a physicalist without committing to any such local supervenience thesis.[14]

PSV* can be seen as a physicalist version of a more general thesis to which all monist theories are committed. The more general thesis could be stated as follows, where *n* is the unified, substantive, fundamental nature that, according to monism, all concrete, actual phenomena share:

> *Supervenience thesis (SV*).* Any possible world that is a minimal *n*-duplicate of the actual world is a duplicate simpliciter of the actual world.

For idealism and neutral monism, the relevant supervenience theses could be stated as follows, where "mental*" refers to fundamental mental phenomena and "neutral*" refers to fundamental neutral phenomena:

> *Idealist supervenience thesis (ISV*).* Any world that is a minimal mental* duplicate of the actual world is a duplicate simpliciter of the actual world.

> *Neutral monist supervenience thesis (NSV*).* Any world that is a minimal neutral* duplicate of the actual world is a duplicate simpliciter of the actual world.

[13] Burge (1979, 1982, 2003) restricts externalism's scope to propositional attitudes, such as beliefs and desires (and he calls the view "anti-individualism"). Dretske (1995), Ball (2009), and Tye (2009) do not. They argue that externalism is true of states of phenomenal consciousness. They also combine externalism with physicalism, which is another position Burge rejects. He writes, "I am no type of physicalist or materialist" (Burge 2010, p. 249).

[14] According to Zhong (2021, p. 1540), "most physicalists agree that mental properties don't individually supervene on physical properties," and by "individually supervene" he seems to mean what I mean by "locally supervene." Zhong provides no evidence for his claim (and I am skeptical). But rejecting local supervenience is at least an option for physicalists.

There is a dualist version of SV* too:

> *Dualist supervenience thesis (DSV*).* Any world that is a minimal mental*-and-physical* duplicate of the actual world is a duplicate simpliciter of the actual world.

Versions could be formulated for other forms of pluralism as well. For example, a version corresponding to a theory that posits three fundamental natures, *N1–N3*, would say: any world that is a minimal *N1-and-N2-and-N3* duplicate of the actual world is a duplicate simpliciter of the actual world. But I will focus on monist versions.[15]

3. Explaining Supervenience

Arguably, supervenience and monism are connected. For example, the physicalist's commitment to mental–physical supervenience can be seen as reflecting her view that, just like everything else in the actual, concrete world, mental phenomena are fundamentally physical. This suggests a third argument for the monism-matters thesis: considerations about monism matter because they help explain why the main monist theories entail certain supervenience theses, for example, why physicalism entails PSV* and why idealism entails ISV*. In standard form:

The Argument from Explaining Supervenience

1. Physicalism, idealism, and neutral monism entail certain supervenience theses.
2. Those theories have those entailments at least partly because they are versions of monism.
3. If (i) physicalism, idealism, and neutral monism entail certain supervenience theses and (ii) those theories have those entailments at least partly because they are versions of monism, then the monism-matters thesis is true.
4. Therefore, the monism-matters thesis is true.

[15] Although physicalism, dualism, idealism, and neutral monism each entail their own supervenience theses, those theses might be compatible with more than one of those theories. For example, arguably neutral monism is consistent with PSV*. See Chapter 7, Section 3.

That argument is valid. Is it sound? I think so. All three premises are plausible. Premise 3 is plausible on its face. The theories in question (physicalism, idealism, and neutral monism) are central to the mind-body debate, and the supervenience theses that they entail reflect their core commitments. Plausibly, if considerations about monism help explain why those theories entail those supervenience theses, then the monism-matters thesis follows, that is, then considerations about monism figure importantly in the contemporary mind-body debate.

The plausibility of premises 1 and 2 can be shown by spelling out some implications of monism as follows:

The Argument from Monism to Supervenience

I. Monism entails MT, which says that all actual, concrete phenomena are such that there is exactly one unified, substantive, fundamental nature *n* that they share.

II. MT entails that no actual, concrete phenomena are over and above *n*-phenomena.

III. If no actual, concrete phenomena are over and above *n*-phenomena, then all actual, concrete phenomena supervene on *n*-phenomena.

IV. Therefore, monism entails that all actual, concrete phenomena supervene on *n*-phenomena.

Before assessing that argument, let me explain how it supports premises 1 and 2 of the Argument from Explaining Supervenience. Assume The Argument from Monism to Supervenience is sound. If we also assume that physicalism, idealism, and neutral monism are versions of monism, then premise 1 of the Argument from Explaining Supervenience ("Physicalism, idealism, and neutral monism entail certain supervenience theses") follows directly. For example, consider idealist monism, according to which *n* is *mental*. If IV (the conclusion of The Argument from Monism to Supervenience) is true, then idealist monism entails that all actual, concrete phenomena supervene on mental phenomena. Likewise for the physicalist and neutral monist versions of monism, *mutatis mutandis*. Further, the assumption that physicalism, idealism, and neutral monism are versions of monism is central to that reasoning. Therefore, premise 2 of The Argument from Explaining Supervenience ("Those theories have those entailments at least partly because they are versions of monism") is also supported: those theories entail supervenience theses at least partly because they are versions of monism, if The Argument from Monism to Supervenience is sound.

Here two remarks are in order.[16] First, my claim that considerations about monism help explain why physicalism, idealism, and neutral monism entail supervenience theses does not rule out the possibility that the entailment could be explained in other ways. Second, monism has different aspects, which are reflected in the various parts of MT: the substantiveness requirement, the unity requirement, etc. Thus, even if considerations about monism help explain why physicalism, idealism, and neutral monism entail supervenience theses, it does not follow that every aspect of monism plays an explanatory role. In particular, it is not clear that the unity requirement does. Imagine a modified version of The Argument from Monism to Supervenience in which MT is replaced by the thesis that all actual, concrete phenomena are such that there is exactly one substantive, fundamental nature that they share—a nature that might or might not be unified. Would the argument still go through? I see no reason to doubt that it would. So, MT's unity requirement might not play any role in The Argument from Monism to Supervenience.

The Argument from Monism to Supervenience is valid. Is it sound? I think so. I argued for premise I ("Monism entails MT") in Chapter 1, Section 1. Premise II ("MT entails that no phenomena are over and above *n*-phenomena") is a conceptual truth based on the close relationship between MT and being over and above. Consider the physicalist version of MT, on which all actual, concrete phenomena are fundamentally physical. How could all such phenomena be fundamentally physical if some are over and above the physical? If *x* is over and above the physical, then, by definition, *x*'s fundamental nature is not wholly physical.

Here I assume that "*x* is nothing over and above y" is neutral on whether *x* and *y* are numerically identical. For example, consider the physicalist's nothing-over-and-above thesis: no actual, concrete phenomena are over and above the physical. I take that thesis to be equally compatible with a familiar type-identity thesis, on which mental-state types are numerically identical to neural-state types (Place 1956, Smart 1959, Lewis 1966, Armstrong 1968), and with the denial of that type-identity thesis (Putnam 1967, Boyd 1980, Pereboom 2002, 2011).

One might instead understand "*x* is nothing over and above *y*" to entail that *x* and *y* are numerically identical. In that case, premise II ("MT entails

[16] Analogous remarks apply to the arguments for the monism-matters thesis that I will present in Chapter 5, Section 1 and Chapter 6, Sections 1–3.

that no phenomena are over and above *n*-phenomena") would be less plausible. But premise II is merely one way of expressing an immediate consequence of MT, and that consequence could be expressed in other ways. For example, we could say, "MT entails that all actual, concrete phenomena *are, or are grounded entirely in*, *n*-phenomena," or "MT entails that all actual, concrete phenomena *exist solely in virtue of the existence of* *n*-phenomena." However, for stylistic convenience, I will usually stick with the "nothing over and above" locution and stipulate that "*x* is nothing over and above y" is neutral on whether *x* and *y* are numerically identical.[17]

Premise III ("If no actual, concrete phenomena are over and above *n*-phenomena, then all actual, concrete phenomena supervene on *n*-phenomena") is another conceptual truth, based on the close relationship between supervenience and being over and above (or between supervenience and being grounded entirely in, or existing in virtue of, etc.). D. Gene Witmer expresses the relevant connection with respect to propositions P and Q as follows:

> ... suppose it is possible for it to be true that Q, while not true that P. Then something in addition to the fact that Q is needed to make it true that P, in which case, surely, the fact that P *is* something over and above the fact that (Witmer 2001, p. 58; italics in original; cf. Loewer 2001, p. 39; Chalmers 1996, 2010).[18]

Essentially the same point could be made with respect to *x*-truths (truths about *x*'s) and *y*-truths (truths about *y*'s). If it is possible for all *x*-truths to obtain without some *y*-truths obtaining—that is, if some *y*-truths do not supervene on *x*-truths—then some *y*-truths would be over and above *x*-truths. Contrapositively: if no *y*-truths are over and above *x*-truths, then all *y*-truths supervene on *x*-truths. Making appropriate substitutions ("truths about *n*-phenomena" for "*x*-truths" and "truths about actual, concrete phenomena" for "*y*-truths") yields a truth-oriented version of premise III: if no

[17] I do not mean to imply that "nothing over and above," "are or are grounded entirely in," and "exist solely in virtue of" are synonymous. My point is rather that, for present purposes, it is enough if MT entails something in the vicinity of the claim that no actual, concrete phenomena are over and above *n*-phenomena.

[18] The claim that *y* is over and above *x* is usually made in cases where *x* and *y* are closely related in some way, but exactly how they relate is in dispute. If Witmer's reasoning is sound, then claims of that form have more general application. In his example, P would be over and above Q even if P and Q are wholly unrelated contingent facts.

truths about actual, concrete phenomena are over and above truths about *n*-phenomena, then all truths about actual, concrete phenomena supervene on truths about *n*-phenomena.

Further support for premise III can be provided by adapting Kripke's (1972, pp. 153–55) creation myth. Kripke reasons roughly as follows. Imagine God creating the world. Suppose God creates C-fiber stimulation, a brain process once thought to be a candidate for a physical phenomenon with which pain could be identified.[19] Must God do further work in order to create pain? If so, then the relation between the types *C-fiber stimulation* and *pain* is not identity. That is Kripke's conclusion. Plausibly, it also follows that pain would be over and above C-fiber stimulation. That idea generalizes: if creating *x*-phenomena is not modally sufficient for creating *y*-phenomena, then *y*-phenomena are over and above *x*-phenomena. And this point about the implications of creation (that is, of whether creating *x*-phenomena suffices for creating *y*-phenomena) suggests a similar point about the implications of supervenience (that is, of whether *y*-phenomena supervene on *x*-phenomena): if some *y*-phenomena do not supervene on *x*-phenomena, then some *y*-phenomena are over and above *x*-phenomena. Contrapositively, if no *y*-phenomena are over and above *x*-phenomena, then all *y*-phenomena supervene on *x*-phenomena. Premise III ("If no actual, concrete phenomena are over and above *n*-phenomena, then all actual, concrete phenomena supervene on *n*-phenomena") is an instance of that universal generalization.

4. Conclusion

In this chapter, I presented two arguments for the monism-matters thesis: The Motivation Argument and The Argument from Explaining Supervenience. According to the former, considerations about monism matter because of their relevance to (i) how the main traditional theories (physicalism, dualism, idealism, and neutral monism) are formulated and (ii) which of those theories, if any, is true. Regarding (i), those theories are traditionally formulated as versions of monism or dualism. Regarding (ii), considerations about monism bear on several arguments for and against physicalism, such

[19] C-fibers are nerve fibers than transmit signals associated with dull, burning, or aching pain. So, strictly speaking, C-fiber stimulation was only ever a candidate for being identified with pain of those kinds.

as parsimony arguments for physicalism, causal arguments for physicalism and against dualism, and The Conceivability Argument against physicalism. According to The Argument from Explaining Supervenience, considerations about monism matter because they help explain why physicalism, idealism, and neutral monism entail supervenience theses, such as the physicalist's PSV*: any world that is a minimal physical* duplicate of our world is a duplicate simpliciter of our world.

I also noted five points about the content of those supervenience theses. First, the supervenience base arguably includes only the most basic phenomena. For example, for the physicalist version, the base would include only microphysical phenomena, if the most basic physical phenomena are all microphysical. Second, each of the relevant supervenience theses includes a minimality constraint, which restricts the scope of the relevant supervenience theses to worlds that contain nothing in addition to those basic phenomena and phenomena thereby necessitated. That makes those theses compatible with the claim that physicalism and its rivals are contingent theses. For example, because PSV* includes a minimality clause, PSV* is compatible with the existence of possible worlds that contain non-physical ghosts. Third, the relevant supervenience theses are not epistemic but rather alethic. Fourth, the relevant sort of alethic necessity is metaphysical (necessity *tout court*) rather than, for example, natural (necessity relativized to natural laws). Fifth, those theses concern global supervenience, not local supervenience.

4
Disorderly Worlds

In Chapter 3, Section 3, I presented The Argument from Explaining Supervenience: considerations about monism matter to the mind-body debate because they help explain why physicalism, idealism, and neutral monism entail supervenience theses. In this chapter, I will address objections to that argument.

1. Is monism superfluous?

One might try to resist The Argument from Explaining Supervenience by objecting as follows:

> Monism is Superfluous
>
> The only role considerations about monism play in The Argument from Explaining Supervenience is to help explain why that physicalism, idealism, and neutral monism entail nothing-over-and-above claims. But considerations about monism are not needed to explain those entailments. Instead, we can think of those nothing-over-and-above claims as deriving from how those theories are defined. For example, it is true by definition that physicalism entails that no concrete phenomena are over and above physical phenomena. Thus, with respect to explaining why physicalism, idealism, and neutral monism entail supervenience theses, considerations about monism are superfluous.

In response, I grant that the relevant nothing-over-and-above claim is often built into the definition of physicalism. The same could be said of idealism and neutral monism. But that just raises the question of why those theories should be defined in that way. Why not define those theories without any such commitment? Indeed, some believe that doing so is called for. In the context of discussing "the idea that physicalists must reject the view that the mental is 'over and above' the fundamental physical realm," Montero and

Monism Matters. Torin Alter, Oxford University Press. © Torin Alter 2026.
DOI: 10.1093/9780198931560.003.0005

Christopher Devlin Brown (2018, p. 530) write, "But what's so bad about one domain of entities being over and above another?" In their view, the physicalist need not find anything bad about that, that is, physicalism need not entail a nothing-over-and-above claim of the relevant sort.[1] Similar reasoning might be applied to idealism and neutral monism. Evidently, the entailments from those theories to the relevant nothing-over-and-above claims require justification. Considerations about monism help in that regard. They are not superfluous. Indeed, one might argue that the relevant nothing-over-and-above claims derive directly from the theories' being versions of monism. For example, part of what it means for everything to share the same fundamental physical nature is that nothing is over and above the physical.

2. Montero's disorderly world

Premise 1 of The Argument from Explaining Supervenience says that physicalism, idealism, and neutral monism entail supervenience theses. In the case of physicalism, the relevant supervenience thesis is PSV* or something similar. (PSV* says: any world that is a minimal physical* duplicate of our world is a duplicate simpliciter of our world.) But according to Montero (2013), physicalism does not entail "restricted supervenience" ("RS"), according to which everything supervenes on "the entities, properties, relations, and laws posited by the physical sciences" (Montero 2013, p. 96). And RS is roughly equivalent to PSV*.

Montero argues for her non-entailment conclusion by devising an alleged counterexample: a coherent scenario in which physicalism could be true even though RS is false. She writes,

> . . . imagine that the world were not generally ordered by supervenience relations, that, for example, neither chemistry nor botany nor bacteriology nor mycology had a supervenience base. Physicalists, in such a situation, should be able to say: "That's just the way the physical world is." In other words, such a disorderly world, though inconsistent with RS, need not be inconsistent with physicalism. (Montero 2013, p. 103)

[1] As I understand Montero and Brown (2018), their point does not depend on the narrow interpretation of the "nothing over and above" locution that I mentioned in Chapter 3, Section 3, on which "*x* is nothing over and above *y*" is true only if $x = y$.

Call the world Montero asks us to imagine *Montero's Disorderly World.* If her argument is sound, then presumably it applies to PSV* no less than to RS. If we substitute PSV* for RS, we can state her argument in standard form as follows:

The Disorderly World Argument

1 Physicalism could be true of Montero's Disorderly World.
2 If physicalism could be true of Montero's Disorderly World, then physicalism does not entail PSV*.
3 Therefore, physicalism does not entail PSV*.[2]

That argument is valid. Is it sound? I think not. But before raising objections, let me note two points. First, I grant premise 2. In Montero's Disorderly World, there are chemical, botanical, etc., phenomena that do not supervene on physical* phenomena. So, if physicalism could be true of that world, then physicalism and the denial of PSV* are compatible. Second, parallel arguments about idealism, neutral monism, and dualism could also be developed. Recall the idealist analogue of PSV* (from Chapter 3, Section 2):

> *Idealist supervenience thesis (ISV*).* Any world that is a minimal mental* duplicate of our world is a duplicate simpliciter of our world.

An idealist version of the passage quoted above from Montero (2013) could be stated as follows:

> . . . imagine that the world were not generally ordered by supervenience relations, that, for example, neither chemistry nor botany nor bacteriology nor mycology had a supervenience base in a single sort of mental* phenomenon. Idealists, in such a situation, should be able to say: "That's just the way the mental world is." In other words, such a disorderly world, though inconsistent with ISV*, need not be inconsistent with idealism.[3]

[2] Montero and Brown (2018) present an equivalent argument, and Zhong (2021) and Moorfoot (2024) present similar ones. The response I will present in Chapter 4, Section 3 applies to all of those arguments, *mutatis mutandis.* I address other arguments against the supervenience requirement on physicalism in Alter (2023, ch. 12).

[3] Here I assume that idealists accept the existence of chemical, botanical, etc., phenomena and take such phenomena to be fundamentally mental. Idealists might take the same position regarding physical phenomena (Berkeley 1710; Adams 2021).

Call the world thus described *The Disorderly Idealist World.* One might formulate an idealist version of The Disorderly World Argument as follows:

The Disorderly World Argument, Idealist Version

1. Idealism could be true of The Disorderly Idealist World.
2. If idealism could be true of The Disorderly Idealist World, then idealism does not entail ISV*.
3. Therefore, idealism does not entail ISV*.

We could also formulate parallel arguments purporting to show that neutral monism and dualism do not entail the neutral monist and dualist analogues of PSV* (which are stated in Chapter 3, Section 2). I will focus on the physicalist version of The Disorderly World Argument. But my criticisms apply equally to the other versions, *mutatis mutandis.*

3. Supervenience and disorder

The problem with The Disorderly World Argument is premise 1, which says that physicalism could be true of Montero's Disorderly World. That premise runs afoul of physicalism's monist commitments. In Montero's Disorderly World, chemical, botanical, etc., phenomena lack a supervenience base. That would seem to entail that, in that world, there is no unified, substantive fundamental nature *n* such that all actual, concrete phenomena supervene on *n*-phenomena. For if there were such a nature *n*, then *n* would serve as a supervenience base for chemical, botanical, etc., phenomena. In other words, premise 1 entails that monism is false of that world. Given that physicalism is a version of monism, it follows that physicalism cannot be true of that world: premise 1 is false.

This can be shown by extending The Argument from Monism to Supervenience (from Chapter 3, Section 3) as follows:

The Argument from Monism to Supervenience, Extended Version

I. Monism entails MT, which says that all actual, concrete phenomena are such that there is exactly one unified, substantive, fundamental nature *n* that they share.
II. MT entails that no actual, concrete phenomena are over and above *n*-phenomena.

III. If no actual, concrete phenomena are over and above n-phenomena, then all actual, concrete phenomena supervene on n-phenomena.
IV. Therefore, monism entails that all actual, concrete phenomena supervene on n-phenomena [from I, II, and III].
V. In Montero's Disorderly World, it is not the case that there is a unified, substantive nature n such that all actual, concrete phenomena supervene on n-phenomena.
VI. Therefore, monism cannot be true of Montero's Disorderly World [from IV and V].
VII. Physicalism is a version of monism.
VIII. Therefore, physicalism cannot be true of Montero's Disorderly World [from VI and VII].

The conclusion of that argument is the denial of premise 1 of The Disorderly World Argument. I conclude that the latter is unsound. Arguably, that reasoning generalizes: the close connections between physicalism and monism, and between monism and supervenience theses such as PSV*, stand in the way of any attempt to deny that physicalism entails PSV*.

In response, Montero might deny that physicalism need be a version of monism. Indeed, there is reason to think she would. She suggests that physicalism ought to be understood in ways that emphasize naturalism or atheism, neither of which need entail monism (Montero 2013, pp. 107–10). For example, she writes, "questions about the existence of God" are "the physicalist's core concern" (Montero 2013, p. 110). But that response does not seem adequate. For one thing, in this book I offer several arguments that put pressure on the idea that physicalism can be detached from monism. For example, in Chapter 3, Section 1, I argued that considerations about monism figure significantly in some of the main arguments for physicalism, including parsimony arguments and causal arguments. Also, physicalism's association with atheism and naturalism is somewhat loose. For example, non-physicalist theories come in atheistic and naturalistic varieties. A prominent example of the latter is Chalmers's (1996, ch. 4) naturalistic dualism, on which the mental supervenes on the physical not with metaphysical necessity but rather in virtue of contingent, natural laws.[4] And his naturalistic

[4] Chalmers does not commit to naturalistic dualism. But he does regard it as "a reasonable and palatable view" (Chalmers 1996, p. 171).

dualism could be combined with atheism. It may also be possible to combine physicalism with theism and non-naturalism.[5]

Montero might be using "physicalism" in a non-traditional way, such that the view lacks its traditional association with monism. But then she is not challenging the received view that physicalism entails a supervenience thesis such as PSV* so much as encouraging a change of subject. In any case, using "physicalism" in a non-traditional way does not resolve the main mind–body issues. For example, we will still wonder whether zombie worlds are ideally conceivable and whether their ideal conceivability entails their possibility (Chalmers 1996, 2010). The only difference would be that The Conceivability Argument would not be directed at physicalism but rather at *schmysicalism*, a version of monism according to which all actual, concrete phenomena share a fundamental physical nature—and which therefore entails PSV*.[6] Such a terminological shift might have advantages, but I see no compelling reason to go that route.[7]

4. Kripke's myth revisited

In Chapter 3, Section 3, I presented an argument modeled on one of Kripke's, based on his creation myth. His argument is sometimes taken to vindicate the claim that physicalism entails a mental-physical supervenience thesis such as PSV*: if creating mental phenomena requires that God do more than create physical phenomena—a scenario that illustrates the denial of mental-physical supervenience—then physicalism is false. Montero and Brown (2018) challenge such Kripke-style reasoning. They do not address the specific Kripke-style argument I presented, which concerns the connection between supervenience and being over-and-above, not the connection between supervenience and physicalism. But if their challenge is cogent, then one might reasonably wonder if a similar challenge could be brought against my argument. However, I will argue, their challenge is not cogent.

[5] See van Inwagen (1978, 1990, 1995). Physicalism might be compatible with theism and non-naturalism if physicalism concerns only concrete phenomena: God might be construed as abstract and not part of nature.

[6] Cf. Kripke (1972, p. 108).

[7] For further discussion of Montero's argument and of related arguments by Montero and Brown (2018) and Zhong (2021), see Alter (2023, ch. 12).

Montero and Brown write:

> Physicalists who accept the "all-God-had-to-do" metaphor do not think that God actually enters the picture. Rather, God is understood as a placeholder for certain unknown forces of nature or chance or whatever it is on nontheological grounds that brought our world into existence. So as long as God does not really exist, what is wrong with having her do a little extra work? This extra work may appear suspect because it seems to involve further acts of creation, as it were, beyond the initial creation of that extremely hot, swarming soup that emanated from the Big Bang. But if physicalists can accept that nature can take care of the initial creation, it seems that they should be able to accept that, if further work were needed, nature could take care of that as well. How this is done might be rather mysterious to us, at least for now; however, just as with the Big Bang, this need not be a reason to take the results as nonphysical. (Montero and Brown 2018, p. 530; cf. Montero 2013, p. 100)

Let us examine the fifth sentence of that passage:

> But if physicalists can accept that nature can take care of the initial creation, it seems that they should be able to accept that, if further work were needed, nature could take care of that as well.

That sentence belies a misunderstanding about the Kripke-style reasoning at issue. Contrary to what Montero and Brown imply, the question dividing physicalists from their opponents is not whether nature can do all the work needed to create mentality. Although physicalists believe nature can (and does) do that, so do naturalistic dualists. Physicalists and dualists (naturalistic or not) part company over a different issue: whether creating the fundamental ingredients that physicalism allows—physical* phenomena—suffices for creating mental phenomena, such as consciousness or minds. If the ingredients required for creating mentality include anything other than fundamental physical phenomena, then physicalism would be false (assuming mentality exists). That follows even if those other ingredients are part of nature. In summary, the issue is not about who or what does the creating but rather about whether the creation of fundamental physical phenomena is modally sufficient for the creation of mental phenomena. The Kripke-style reasoning in question pertains to the latter issue (about modal sufficiency), not the former one (about who or what does the creating) and is thus not undermined by Montero and Brown's challenge.

5. Supervenience and grounding

In The Argument from Monism to Supervenience (Chapter 3, Section 3), the route from monism to supervenience goes via a nothing-over-and-above claim: "no actual, concrete phenomena are over and above *n*-phenomena." In discussing that argument, I noted that it could instead invoke a different intermediary claim, such as a claim about (metaphysical) grounding. An alternative version could be stated as follows:

The Argument from Monism to Supervenience, Grounding Version

I. Monism entails MT, which says that all actual, concrete phenomena are such that there is exactly one unified, substantive, fundamental nature *n* that they share.

II.′ MT entails that all actual, concrete phenomena are or are wholly grounded in *n*-phenomena.

III.′ If all actual, concrete phenomena are or are wholly grounded in *n*-phenomena, then all actual, concrete phenomena supervene on *n*-phenomena.

IV. Therefore, monism entails that all actual, concrete phenomena supervene on *n*-phenomena.

The Argument from Monism to Supervenience, Grounding Version is valid. Is it sound? I think so. Premise I is unchanged (that is, it is the same as premise I of the unmodified version of The Argument from Monism to Supervenience). Again, I argued for it in Chapter 1, Section 1. Like premises II and III, premises II′ and III′ are conceptual truths, which can be supported in analogous ways. Regarding premise II′, consider the physicalist version of MT, on which all actual, concrete phenomena are fundamentally physical. How could all such phenomena be fundamentally physical* if some are neither physical* nor wholly grounded in physical* phenomena? Regarding premise III′, we could again appeal to Kripke's creation myth. If God's creating *n*-phenomena is not modally sufficient for creating some actual, concrete phenomena, then some actual, concrete phenomena are neither *n*-phenomena nor wholly grounded in *n*-phenomena. Further, premise

III′ follows from the widely held view that grounding entails metaphysical necessitation, that is, (metaphysical) supervenience (Rosen 2010; Audi 2012a; Fine 2012; Dasgupta 2015; O'Conaill 2018).[8]

However, that widely held view has been disputed. Arguments against it have been developed by Stephan Leuenberger (2014) and Alexander Skiles (2015). Their arguments might seem to threaten The Argument from Monism to Supervenience, Grounding Version. Further, one might wonder if parallel arguments would threaten any version of The Argument from Monism to Supervenience. In this section, I will argue that the threat is illusory.

I will begin with some remarks about grounding. Grounding is often described as a relation of *ontological dependence* (Fine 2012) or existing-in-virtue-of (Pereboom 2020). Sometimes grounding takes the form of constitution, as in the case of a diamond's being constituted by a lattice of carbon atoms. Grounding can take other forms as well. For example, a conjunctive truth is grounded in, but perhaps not constituted by, the corresponding conjuncts. I hope those examples convey the basic idea.[9] But I will mention four other points.

First, unless otherwise specified, I have in mind full grounding rather than partial grounding. For example, in the diamond case, the claim is that the diamond is wholly constituted by, and thus grounded entirely in, the lattice of carbon atoms: nothing in addition to the lattice is involved in grounding the diamond. Second, the relevant notion of grounding is synchronic, rather than diachronic. Third, there is a debate about whether "grounding" names a distinctive, unified relation or rather a disjunction of more specific relations, such as constitution, realization, etc. (Wilson 2014). Here I take no stand on that debate. Fourth, x might ground y without being part of y's *ultimate* ground. For example, although a diamond is constituted by carbon atoms, it is not ultimately so constituted: carbon atoms are themselves constituted by more basic entities. Likewise, a complex visual experience might be grounded in simpler visual experiences without being ultimately mentally grounded. For example, suppose a visual experience of the American flag is grounded in experiences of red, of white, and of blue (*pace* Tye 2007). If the experiences of red, etc., are fundamentally non-mental (e.g., if they are wholly physical), then the ultimate ground of the flag experience does not include mentality.

[8] I use "x supervenes on y" and "y necessitates x" interchangeably.

[9] For more details, see Bliss and Trogdon (2021).

Let us turn to Skiles's (2015) argument. He argues for *grounding contingentism*, which says that a fact F can be grounded in a set of facts Γ without supervening on Γ. He bases his argument largely on counterexamples to *grounding necessitarianism*, which says that if Γ grounds F, then F supervenes on Γ. He begins with the idea that an ordinary composite object is grounded in its parts (Conee and Sider 2005, p. 68). He then considers rearrangements of those parts modeled on the ship of Theseus:

> Let "o" pick out a particular tuna sandwich. Suppose that in an earlier epoch, the existence of o is grounded in an arrangement of its parts, the *as* (call this arrangement "Γ"). At a later epoch, one of the *as* (call it "a_1") is sloughed off and replaced with a duplicate (call it "b_1"). There is now a sandwich composed of $b_1, a_2, \ldots a_n$: this sandwich (call it "o_1") is presumably identical to o. Suppose this process of gradual replacement repeats so that eventually in a later epoch, we are left with two sandwiches: one (call it "o_n") identical to o and composed of $b_1, b_2, \ldots, b_n$, but also another sandwich (call it "o_R", for *replacement*) composed of $a_1, a_2, \ldots, a_n$ and placed in the same arrangement, Γ, they were in when they composed o in the *earlier* epoch. Finally, o is destroyed, leaving o_R unscathed. Although all the facts in Γ obtain during this later epoch, [o exists] does not; hence although the existence of o was *grounded* in these facts about its parts, they do not *necessitate* o's existence. (Skiles 2015, p. 722)

What does that case show? It might refute what could be called *local grounding necessitarianism*: a doctrine about one proper part of reality being grounded in another proper part of reality. But the case does not refute *global grounding necessitarianism*, which is all that is relevant here. SV (and PSV* in particular) is a form of global supervenience. It says that any possible world that is a minimal n-duplicate of the actual world is a duplicate simpliciter of the actual world. Skiles's argument has no implications for the relationship between grounding and global supervenience—at least none that threaten my arguments, including The Argument from Monism to Supervenience, Grounding Version. The same is true of Skiles's other counterexamples to grounding necessitarianism. Indeed, Skiles acknowledges that "grounding contingentism is . . . compatible with the global supervenience of every fact on the fundamental facts" (Skiles 2015, p. 738).[10] One should not infer from

[10] Skiles's (2015, p. 738) formulation of global supervenience, with which he says grounding contingentism is compatible, is stronger than SV. Unlike SV, his formulation does not include a minimality constraint. See Chapter 3, Section 3.

the failure of local necessitation that global necessitation fails any more than one should infer from the fact that someone can stand without one foot on the ground that they can stand without any feet on the ground.

One might reply as follows:

> Skiles's tuna-sandwich case shows that grounding does not always entail necessitation. Therefore, it is ad hoc to insist that a global grounding claim requires a global necessitation claim.

But if Skiles's cases involve grounding without necessitation, that is due to features specific to local grounding, for example, features of our concept of a sandwich. It does not follow that it is ad hoc to assume that global grounding entails global supervenience. Further, Skiles's argument depends on the assumption that an ordinary composite object, such as a sandwich, is fully grounded in its parts. One could see his cases as challenging that assumption rather than as establishing even a local version of grounding contingentism.

Let me turn to Leuenberger's arguments. His "main target" is the following claim.

> **Entailment** Necessarily, if $\Gamma < A$ then $\Box(O(\Gamma) \rightarrow O(A))$. (Leuenberger 2014, p. 155, boldface in original)[11]

Here Γ is the set of facts that grounds fact *A*, "<" denotes the grounding relation, "$\Box$" is a metaphysical necessity operator, "*O*(*A*)" and "*O*(Γ)" "express that *A* obtains and that all members of Γ obtain, respectively" (p. 154). Leuenberger presents two arguments against Entailment. I will focus on the one that is most relevant to present concerns.[12]

That argument concerns physicalism, which, according to Leuenberger, entails that all facts, including phenomenal facts (that is, facts about phenomenal consciousness), are grounded in actual physical facts. As an example of a phenomenal fact, he refers to *Red*: "the fact that I am having a

[11] Leuenberger's formulation of Entailment is puzzling. Is the "obtains" operator needed? If so, why isn't there an infinite regress problem of the Lewis Carroll (1895) sort? Does "*O*(Γ)" require another "O" in front of it, which in turn requires another . . . ? Also, why is "Necessarily" included? Isn't the "$\Box$" sufficient to capture the necessitation in question? Neither of these issues is especially relevant here. I will set them aside.

[12] My main objections also apply to Leuenberger's other argument against Entailment, *mutatis mutandis.*

red experience" (Leuenberger 2014, p. 157). He summarizes his argument as follows:

1. Possibly, physicalism is true and *Red* obtains as a non-fundamental fact.
2. Necessarily, there are no physical facts Γ such that $\Box(O(\Gamma) \rightarrow O(Red))$.
3. Necessarily, if physicalism is true, then for every non-fundamental fact A there are physical facts Γ such that $\Gamma < A$.

From these premises, it follows (even in a very weak modal logic) that it is not necessary that for all Γ, if $\Gamma < Red$ then $\Box(O(\Gamma) \rightarrow O(Red))$, and hence that Entailment has a false instance (Leuenberger 2014, p. 157).

Leuenberger's argument is valid. But premises 1 and 2 lack adequate support and face dialectical objections. Put in terms of possible worlds, premise 1 asserts that there is a possible world in which all fundamental facts are physical and yet *Red* ("the fact that I am having a red experience") obtains. But the latter conjunction is precisely the sort of claim that divides physicalists and their opponents, such as dualists. According to physicalists, the fundamental physical facts are sufficient for *Red* to obtain. Dualists disagree. They argue that there would have to be further, non-physical facts in order for *Red* to obtain.[13] So, in the context of the debate over what physicalism entails, premise 1 requires independent support: support that should be convincing to a neutral party, that is, to someone who is committed to neither physicalism nor the denial of physicalism. Leuenberger provides no such independent support. Nor does he engage with the arguments that anti-physicalists present against claims such as premise 1.

Leuenberger considers the objection I just presented (or something close to it). He labels it "the objection from dualism" and suggests that it is dialectically problematic. In his view, to bring it against his argument, one would have to be "saddle[d] . . . with a commitment to the falsity of physicalism" (Leuenberger 2014, p. 158)—and thus beg the question against physicalism. But that is not so. One need not assume that physicalism is false in order to recognize that premise 1 requires support of a kind that Leuenberger does not provide. The problem arises because opponents of physicalism, including dualists, deny that premise. To assert premise 1 without either providing independent support or engaging with arguments against that premise is, in effect, to assume that dualism is false. Such reasoning should

[13] Here I assume, for simplicity, that there are fundamental facts that ground all non-fundamental facts. But see Chapter 5, Section 4.

seem unconvincing not just to dualists but to those who are neutral regarding physicalism's truth or falsity.

A parallel problem arises for premise 2 (which says that, necessarily, there are no physical facts that necessitate *Red*). That premise is controversial in the mind–body literature. Indeed, even the weaker premise with the initial "necessarily" removed ("there are no physical facts that necessitate *Red*") is controversial. It requires substantial independent support. Leuenberger provides little. He merely asserts that it is conceivable for the physical facts to obtain while *Red* does not, that this conceivability appears to entail the corresponding possibility, and that "we have no particular reason to think that the appearance of possibility is misleading in this case" (Leuenberger 2014, p. 157). But as he concedes, "it is hard to substantiate these claims" (Leuenberger 2014, p. 158). Moreover, in the context of the debate over what physicalism entails, the plausibility of those claims—claims that physicalists reject—cannot be taken for granted.

Leuenberger considers that objection (or something close to it) too, and his response parallels his response to the objection to premise 1. He misdescribes the objection, labeling it "the objection from necessitarianism," and suggests that it rests on a controversial necessitarian doctrine on which "metaphysical possibility is just logical compatibility with the laws of nature" (Leuenberger 2014, p. 158). But the objection rests on no such doctrine. The objection is that he bases premise 2 on controversial claims that he fails to justify. Once again, it is Leuenberger's reasoning that is dialectically problematic, not his opponent's.

Leuenberger gives another argument that is worth considering here. He argues that physicalism is compatible with the possibility of a zombie world.[14] PSV* rules out that possibility (assuming consciousness actually exists). Therefore, if Leuenberger were correct that physicalism is compatible with that possibility, then physicalism does not entail PSV*.

Leuenberger's argument involves the following variant of Kripke's creation myth:

> In the actual world, God had put all the physical facts in place by the end of day seven. This was enough to make it the case that *Red* obtains. God henceforth left the world alone. In world w_b, God on day eight ensured that

[14] Leuenberger develops that argument in response to an objection to the compatibility of his premises 1 and 2. But it could as easily be seen as an independent argument against Entailment. Anyway, this does not affect my criticisms.

> in the region occupied by my brain, a non-physical fundamental property, to be called 'chromaplasm', is instantiated. Chromaplasm makes visual phenomenology disappear. In w_b, I do not have a red experience, i.e. *Red* does not hold. (Leuenberger 2014, p. 160)

As Leuenberger (2014, p. 160) states, physicalism is not true of w_b "because of the presence of chromaplasm." But he supposes that physicalism is true of the actual world anyway:

> Since in the actual world, God only created physical facts and then retired, physicalism is true. All the actual fundamental facts are physical, after all, and that seems to be sufficient condition for the truth of physicalism. Hence *Red* is grounded by some class of physical facts. (Leuenberger 2014, p. 161)

Leuenberger's argument has at least two problems. First, it is problematic in the same way that premises 1 and 2 of his other argument are. In describing his variant of Kripke's creation myth, he writes that God's creating the physical facts "was enough to make it the case that *Red* obtains." But in the context of the mind-body debate, that sufficiency claim is one that divides physicalists and their opponents. It cannot simply be asserted without providing justification.

Second, the supervenience thesis to which physicalists are committed includes a minimality condition, that is, a condition specifying that the relevant duplicate worlds contain nothing in addition to the same (or exactly similar) physical phenomena that the actual world contains. Jackson's (1998) formulation of the physicalist's supervenience thesis makes that minimality condition explicit (indeed, "minimal" is italicized): "Any world which is a *minimal* physical duplicate of our world is a duplicate *simpliciter* of our world" (Jackson 1998, p. 12, italics in original). Although w_b is a physical duplicate of the actual world, it is not a minimal physical duplicate, due to the presence of chromaplasm. So, the scenario Leuenberger describes is not one where the physicalist's grounding claim is true while her supervenience thesis is false.

Thus, neither Skiles's nor Leuenberger's arguments establish the compatibility of the physicalist's grounding claim with the denial of a relevant supervenience thesis, such as PSV*. Nor do their arguments undermine The Argument from Monism to Supervenience, Grounding Version or any other argument I have given.

6. Conclusion

According to The Argument from Explaining Supervenience, considerations about monism matter because they help explain why the main traditional monist theories—physicalism, idealism, and neutral monism—entail supervenience theses. In this chapter, I defended that entailment against three objections: that considerations about monism are not needed to explain that entailment; that there is no such entailment; and that my assumption that grounding entails supervenience is false. I argued that all three objections trace to misunderstandings about the commitments of physicalism and its rivals—commitments that derive at least partly from those theories' being versions of monism.

5
Monism and Repudiation

In Chapter 3, I presented two arguments for the monism-matters thesis, and I defended one of them in Chapter 4. In this chapter, I will present a third: considerations about monism help explain why traditional versions of monism entail certain repudiation theses, such as the physicalist thesis that there is no fundamental mentality. I will also consider alleged counterexamples to that thesis and argue that they fail.

1. Explaining repudiation

A *repudiation thesis* is a thesis repudiating a certain type of phenomenon as a fundamental component of the universe. Physicalists repudiate fundamentally mental phenomena and fundamentally neutral phenomena.[1] Idealists repudiate fundamentally physical phenomena and fundamentally neutral phenomena. And neutral monists repudiate fundamentally mental phenomena and fundamentally physical phenomena. Why do physicalism, idealism, and neutral monism entail those repudiation theses? Part of the answer, I contend, is that each theory is a version of monism. If so, that provides another argument for the monism-matters thesis:

The Argument from Explaining Repudiation

1. Physicalism, idealism, and neutral monism entail certain repudiation theses.
2. Those theories have those entailments at least partly because they are versions of monism.
3. If (i) physicalism, idealism, and neutral monism entail certain repudiation theses and (ii) those theories have those entailments at least partly

[1] The existence of fundamental mental phenomena is consistent with the theory Strawson (2008) calls "real materialism." Indeed, he argues that their existence is entailed by that theory. But here my concern is with physicalism as it is standardly understood, and Strawson's theory does not fit that description. See fn. 6, Chapter 2.

Monism Matters. Torin Alter, Oxford University Press. © Torin Alter 2026.
DOI: 10.1093/9780198931560.003.0006

because they are versions of monism, then the monism-matters thesis is true.

4. Therefore, the monism-matters thesis is true.

That argument is valid. Is it sound? I think so. Premise 3 is plausible, given the plausible assumptions that physicalism, idealism, and neutral monism are significant to the mind-body debate and that the entailed repudiation theses represent important commitments of those theories. Premises 1 and 2 are also plausible, as I will now argue.

I will start with premise 2 ("Those theories have those entailments at least partly because they are versions of monism"). Consider physicalism's repudiation of fundamental mentality. How should that be explained? A plausible explanation runs as follows. Physicalism entails the physicalist version of MT: all actual, concrete phenomena are such that there is exactly one unified, substantive, fundamental nature that they share, and that shared nature is physical, that is, physical *as opposed to* mental (or neutral). It follows that no actual, concrete phenomena are fundamentally mental. Parallel reasoning applies to the idealist's and the neutral monist's repudiation theses.

I will elaborate on that explanation in response to the following objection:

> If monist theories entail repudiation theses, then this is only because of how we choose to define those theories. For example, we choose to define physicalism so as to be incompatible with the existence of fundamental mentality. However, the objector contends, that choice is arbitrary.

Do physicalists have a non-arbitrary reason to repudiate fundamental mentality? If so, is monism implicated? The answer to both questions is *yes*. Here it will be instructive to consider mentality that physicalists need not repudiate. For example, consider a sort of mentality recognized by physicalists who are realizer functionalists. Those philosophers identify mental properties with lower-order properties that realize certain higher-order functional properties (or that satisfy certain higher-order functional descriptions), relative to a certain population. On one version of that theory, advocated by David K. Lewis (1966) and David M. Armstrong (1968), mental properties in humans are identified with certain neural properties. For example, in humans, physical pain might be identified with a neural property *N* (e.g., C-fiber stimulation) on the grounds that *N* realizes a functional property that could be expressed roughly as "the state that is typically caused by damage to the body and that typically causes the person to exhibit behavior such as grimacing, etc." *N* is mental, but not fundamentally. *N* is a brain state. It is fundamentally physical. That is why physicalists accept its existence. But they would not accept the existence of any fundamentally mental phenomenon. Why not?

A plausible answer runs as follows. As a version of monism, physicalism entails that there is exactly one substantive, unified, fundamental nature that all actual, concrete phenomena share, and that nature is physical, not mental. Unlike the mentality recognized by realizer-functionalist physicalists, fundamentally mental phenomena would not consist in the physical realization of higher-order functional properties. On the contrary, fundamentally mental phenomena would not be physical. Nor would they be realized by (or grounded in) physical phenomena. A fundamentally mental phenomenon is exactly the sort of thing physicalists do not countenance: something that is over and above the physical.

For similar, monism-based reasons, physicalists cannot countenance the existence of fundamentally neutral phenomena. Parallel reasoning also helps explain why idealists and neutral monists are also committed to certain repudiation theses. For example, idealists cannot countenance the existence of fundamentally physical phenomena because, as a version of monism, idealism says the actual, concrete universe contains only fundamentally mental phenomena. Thus, premise 2 is plausible: physicalism, idealism, and neutral monism entail certain repudiation theses at least partly because they are versions of monism.[2]

In light of the monism-based argument that I just gave for premise 2, premise 1 ("Physicalism, idealism, and neutral monism entail certain repudiation theses") might seem to require no further defense. But that is not so, at least with respect to the claim that physicalists must repudiate fundamentally mental phenomena. Though widely accepted, that claim has received considerable pushback (Lewis 1983; Chomsky 1995; Stoljar 2022; Dowell 2006; Strawson 2008). Indeed, according to some philosophers, there are counterexamples: coherent scenarios in which physicalism might be true despite the existence of fundamental mentality (Dorsey 2011; Zhong 2016; Brown 2021, 2023). I will argue that those alleged counterexamples are based on a misunderstanding of the physicalist's repudiation of fundamental

[2] This is not to say that only monist theories entail repudiation theses. Some non-monist theories do too. For example, Cartesian dualism entails that there are no fundamentally neutral phenomena.

mentality. But first I will provide some context and explain how the counterexamples are supposed to work.

2. Wilson's No Fundamental Mentality constraint

Discussions about physicalism and fundamental mentality often begin with a problem we encountered in Chapter 2, Section 4: Hempel's dilemma. Hempel's dilemma arises for attempts to define the physical by reference to physical theory. Defining the physical by reference to current physical theory is problematic because that theory is incomplete. Defining the physical by reference to ideal physical theory is problematic because we do not know that theory's contents. In particular, for all we know, it posits something mental, such as consciousness. Yet to most physicalists, fundamental mental phenomena are considered anathema.

As I noted in Chapter 2, Section 7, Wilson addresses that last problem with her No Fundamental Mentality (NFM) constraint. The idea is to stipulate that the physical does not include fundamentally mental phenomena. That way, there is no danger of something fundamentally mental qualifying as physical, even if ideal physics posits such a thing. But that raises a further question: what justifies that stipulation? Why isn't doing so ad hoc?

Wilson provides an answer:

> Reflecting the historical roots of physicalism in materialism as foundationally committed to understanding mentality as nothing over and above complex material goings on, one feature has remained definitive of the term 'physical': namely, that the compositionally basic physical entities and features are not fundamentally mental—that is, do not individually either possess or bestow mentality. (Wilson 2021, p. 23; cf. Wilson 2005, p. 428, 2006)

I will return to this in Section 4, after explaining the alleged counterexamples in Section 3.[3]

[3] Although Wilson introduces her NFM constraint as a constraint on the physical, it is often taken to be a constraint on physical*ism*, that is, as (what I call) the physicalist's repudiation thesis: the thesis that physicalism is incompatible with the existence of fundamentally mental phenomena (Brown 2023). I use "the NFM constraint" in both ways. Sometimes I use it as Wilson does, to refer to a restriction on the class of physical phenomena. Sometimes I use it as others do, to refer to a restriction on physicalism, that is, as equivalent to the claim that physicalism repudiates the existence of fundamental mentality. Context will disambiguate.

3. Alleged counterexamples

Jonathan Dorsey (2011) writes:

> Suppose you are operating an atom smasher and you think you have discovered a physical simple, i.e. a physical entity with no proper parts. You discover it has certain properties, like (say) spin, mass, certain effects on quarks, a definite spatial location when measured, and so forth. But, now, imagine God pays you a visit, assuring you this thing is indeed a simple but also that it has a mental property. (Dorsey 2011, p. 219)

How should we describe the entity that you discover? Dorsey suggests that it is both physical and fundamentally mental. That sounds like exactly what the NFM constraint would rule out as impossible. Yet the scenario he describes seems coherent. He concludes that the NFM constraint should be rejected.

Lei Zhong (2016) describes two scenarios that seem to pose a similar threat to the NFM constraint. One involves a hypothetical phenomenon he calls "S-neutrino fluctuation": a fundamental microphysical phenomenon that "has a non-mental mode of presentation in ideal physics" (Zhong 2016, p. 581). He imagines that S-neutrino fluctuation turns out to be identical to consciousness. The other scenario involves C-fiber stimulation. He writes, "Suppose that ideal physics tells us that C-fibers are fundamental, irreducible entities. And suppose further that pain is identical with C-fiber firing" (Zhong 2016, p. 582). In his view, although both scenarios are consistent with physicalism, the NFM constraint implies otherwise. He concludes that the NFM constraint should be rejected.

Brown writes, "NFM wrongly rules that physicalism is false in certain classes of metaphysically possible worlds" (Brown 2023, p. 2).[4] One class contains "priority monist worlds in which the whole of nature is a mental system which possesses functionally-characterizable mentality" (Brown 2023, p. 2). "Priority monism" is Schaffer's (2010) term for the holist view that the cosmos ("the whole of nature") is fundamental: "the world has parts, but the parts are dependent fragments of an integrated whole" (Schaffer 2010,

[4] To be a counterexample to the NFM constraint, it is not clear that a relevant scenario must be metaphysically possible. One might have thought that coherence, logical consistency, or ideal conceivability would suffice. But we need not settle this matter here. If the scenarios Brown describes are metaphysically possible, then *a fortiori* they are coherent, logically consistent, and ideally conceivable.

p. 33). Brown describes a priority-monist world that he takes to threaten the NFM constraint as follows[5]:

> Imagine a world containing only a single functioning brain. All non-brain entities in this world are parts of the brain—nothing is left floating free in the cosmic void. This brain realizes mental properties, and those mental properties are necessitated by the instantiation of appropriate relational properties of the parts of the brain.... add the detail that priority monism is true in this world, and we get the result that some properties of the cosmos-encompassing brain ... are fundamental. Since this brain has mental properties, some mental properties may be fundamental in this world. (Brown 2021, p. 2850)[6]

Here "appropriate relational properties" might be lower-order realizers of higher-order functional properties. Those realizers might be "physicalism-friendly," that is, compatible with physicalism. By realizer functionalism, such physicalism-friendly properties would qualify as mental. But according to Brown, as instantiated in the priority-monist world he imagines, they might be fundamental.

Brown (2023, p. 3) also imagines "an artificially intelligent (henceforth 'AI') quantum computer which employs quantum properties as part of its cognitive operations." By realizer functionalism, one of those quantum properties might qualify as a physicalism-friendly mental property. Nevertheless, that same quantum property might be fundamental. Thus, Brown concludes, physicalism is compatible with the existence of fundamental mentality, contrary to the NFM constraint.

According to Brown, the challenge his quantum-computer case creates for the NFM constraint is "more troubling than other criticisms" (Brown 2023, p. 3), such as Dorsey's, Zhong's, and his own priority-monism-based criticism. That is because other criticisms are based on cases that rely on "contentious metaphysical assumptions." Those cases, he suggests, might not be

[5] Brown (2021) also describes a variant of that priority-monist world. But most differences between that variant and the world describe in the passage quoted above do not matter here. Those that do are subsumed by the class of worlds I go on to discuss.

[6] It is not clear how that conclusion ("some mental properties may be fundamental in this world") follows. Even given the assumptions that, in the described scenario, priority monism is true and the brain in question is cosmos-encompassing, why think any of its mental properties are fundamental? Brown addresses this concern by criticizing reasons to deny that any of its mental properties could be fundamental. One might challenge that reasoning, but here I set the concern aside.

metaphysically possible. By contrast, he claims, the quantum computer he describes is not only metaphysically possible but nomologically possible. He writes, "I suspect that this counterexample may become actual at some time in the foreseeable future" (Brown 2023, p. 3; cf. Feynman 1982).

What about the assumption that quantum properties are fundamental? Isn't that a contentious metaphysical assumption? Brown recognizes that problem: "Some views in physics, such as string theory, posit even-more-fundamental properties underlying the properties of better-established subatomic theories" (Brown 2023, p. 7). However, he writes,

> . . . it seems fairly reasonable to suppose that quantum mechanical properties or properties that are very similar to them are fundamental... ... however deep the fundamental level lies, it seems a plausible supposition that we might (in principle, anyway) exploit the properties at that level to perform computations. And this is all that my argument requires. (Brown 2023, p. 7).

So, perhaps Brown should say that the artificially intelligent computer he imagines employs quantum mechanical properties *or properties that are very similar to them* as part of its cognitive operations. Either way, he suggests, the relevant properties could be fundamental. I will assume that he is correct about that and henceforth set aside the concern that quantum properties might not be fundamental.

4. Two kinds of fundamental mentality

In the next section, I will argue that the alleged counterexamples described in the preceding section fail to refute Wilson's NFM constraint. But they do force us to get clearer about what her constraint does and does not rule out. In other words, we need to clarify what "fundamental mentality" means in this context. That is the topic of the present section.

Perhaps the general idea is clear enough. As Brown (2021, p. 2843) writes, "Fundamental mentality is mentality which metaphysically depends on nothing else—it is mentality at the bottom of nature..." But that could mean at least two different things.[7] On the one hand, something might count as

[7] The same is true of how Zhong (2016, p. 573, fn. 6) and Wilson (2006, p. 68) characterize fundamental mentality. I discuss Dorsey's (2011) characterization in Section 6.

fundamentally mental if it is mental and exists at the most fundamental level of nature. Call that kind of fundamental mentality *levels based*. On the other hand, something might count as fundamentally mental if it is either primitively mental (mental and ungrounded) or what I will call *quasi-primitively mental*: mentality that is ultimately grounded at least partly in mentality. Call that kind of fundamental mentality (mentality that is either primitively or quasi-primitively mental) *primitive-mentality based*.[8]

Those two notions—levels-based fundamental mentality and primitive-mentality-based fundamental mentality—are not equivalent.[9] Where levels-based fundamental mentality is concerned, the term "fundamental" applies to a level of nature. Here it is assumed that nature is stratified into a hierarchy of levels, where the most fundamental level is that on which all other levels metaphysically depend (Schaffer 2003). For example, the most fundamental level might be the microphysical level, while the chemical level is less fundamental, and the biological level is still less fundamental.[10] On the levels-based approach, fundamental mentality is mentality that exists at the most fundamental level. By contrast, where primitive-mentality-based fundamental mentality is concerned, the term "fundamental" applies not to a level of nature but rather to a type of mentality: primitive or quasi-primitive mentality, that is, mentality that admits of no analysis in non-mental terms.

The distinction between levels-based fundamental mentality and primitive-mentality-based fundamental mentality yields two different versions of the NFM constraint.[11] There is

> *The levels-based NFM constraint*. Physicalism is incompatible with the existence of levels-based fundamental mentality.

[8] Although I characterize primitive-mentality-based fundamental mentality partly in terms of grounding, this is not essential. The point is that if x is fundamentally mental in this sense, then x is irreducibly mental or at least entails the existence of irreducible mentality. In other words, x admits of no analysis in non-mental terms.

[9] What if a "fundamental level" were defined as a level on which no entities are grounded in anything else? Would that erase the distinction between levels-based fundamental mentality and primitive-mentality-based fundamental mentality? Perhaps. But that is not the way Brown et al., use the term "fundamental level." Again, according to Brown, mental phenomena might exist at the most fundamental level even though (indeed, because) they are grounded in physical phenomena.

[10] The bottom level might not be the microphysical level. On Schaffer's (2010) priority monism, it is not. For challenges to the assumption that nature is stratified into a hierarchy of levels, see Heil (2003). Cf. Morris (2019).

[11] Here I take NFM constraint to concern physicalism rather than the physical. See fn. 3.

There is also

> *The primitive-mentality-based NFM constraint.* Physicalism is incompatible with the existence of primitive-mentality-based fundamental mentality.

How should the NFM constraint be understood, as the levels-based version or as the primitive-mentality-based version?[12]

Zhong and Brown seem to favor the levels-based interpretation. For example, Zhong (2016, p. 573) equates fundamental mentality with "mentality [that] exists at the fundamental metaphysical level" (cf. Brown 2023, p. 2, fn. 2). Moreover, all of the alleged counterexamples that I described in Section 3 seem to depend on the levels-based interpretation. They involve physicalism-friendly mentality existing at the most fundamental level of nature. That the mentality in question exists at that level would seem to be why it qualifies as fundamental.

But there are good reasons to interpret the NFM constraint as the primitive-mentality-based version rather than the levels-based version. I will describe four such reasons: one concerning a better fit with physicalism and its rivals, one concerning reductionist physicalism, one concerning panpsychism, and one concerning bottomless worlds.

A better fit. Historically, two of physicalism's main rivals are dualism and idealism, and the primitive-mentality-based version comports better with those rival theories. On dualism and idealism, mentality does not consist in non-mentality of any kind, be it physical or anything else (Robinson 2023; Guyer and Horstmann 2023). On those views, there is primitive (and quasi-primitive) mentality, and levels need not enter the picture. Moreover, recall why physicalists tend to regard fundamental mentality as anathema. As Wilson explains in the passage that I quoted in Section 2, the physicalist's worry about fundamental mentality is that it would be over and above the

[12] It is not entirely clear how Wilson conceives of the sort of fundamental mentality that the NFM constraint concerns. Some remarks could be read as suggesting the levels-based kind, for example, "physicalism is incompatible with . . . the view that mentality exists at relatively low levels of constitutional complexity (that is, those levels treated by fundamental physics)" (Wilson 2005, p. 428). But other remarks suggest the primitive-mentality-based kind. For example, she refers to the sorts of entities whose existence would "falsify physicalism" as "to some degree constituted by mentality" (Wilson 2006, p. 76). There are other indications that support the latter interpretation. For example, she notes that physicalism stands opposed to strong-emergentist views on which there is non-physical mentality at relatively high (that is, non-fundamental) levels of nature (Wilson 2006, p. 69). Such mentality would be fundamental in the primitive-mentality-based sense but not in the levels-based sense.

physical. In other words, if there were fundamental mentality, then mental phenomena would not be grounded solely in physical phenomena. That worry does not concern *where* or *at what level* mentality exists. Instead, the worry concerns the fundamental nature of mentality—the kind of thing it would fundamentally be (Alter 2022). This suggests the primitive-mentality-based interpretation.[13]

Think of it through the prism of physicalist monism. The actual, concrete world contains various and sundry phenomena. There are chemical phenomena, biological phenomena, psychological phenomena, and many other types too. But if physicalist monism is true, then ultimately all of them are fundamentally of a single, unified type, namely, physical. That is, everything is either itself a physical phenomenon or ultimately physically grounded.[14] On this view, although many things are chemically grounded, none is ultimately chemically grounded (or ultimately biologically grounded or . . .). Likewise, nothing is ultimately mentally grounded. Nor is anything both mental and ungrounded. If physicalist monism is true, then mental phenomena are, or are ultimately grounded entirely in, physical phenomena, as opposed to any other type of phenomena—including the mental type. That physicalist claim conflicts with the claim that there is primitive or quasi-primitive mentality. Does that physicalist claim conflict with the claim that mentality exists at the most fundamental level of nature?

No, it does not, at least not clearly. Those two claims concern different issues. The physicalist claim that mental phenomena are, or are ultimately grounded in, physical phenomena concerns the nature of mental phenomena, whereas the claim that mentality exists at the most fundamental level of nature concerns where (at what level) mental phenomena reside. So, there is no direct conflict between the two claims. Nor does there appear to be an indirect conflict. Here it might help to recall the realizer functionalist view of Lewis (1966) and Armstrong (1968). According to Lewis and Armstrong, mental properties are identified with lower-order properties that, in a certain population, realize certain higher-order functional

[13] Here one might object that the term "grounding" implies something about levels, for example, that "x grounds y" implies that x exists at a lower level than y. In response, I concede some might associate the term with something about levels. But as I use the term, that association is not part of its meaning. Also, as I noted above (fn. 8), although I characterize primitive-mentality-based fundamental mentality partly in terms of grounding, this is not essential.

[14] Here I express physicalism partly in terms of grounding (see Chapter 8). But this is inessential to the present point. References to grounding could be considered proxies for whatever relation physicalists believe obtains between physical* phenomena and other actual, concrete phenomena.

properties. For example, in humans, pain might be identified with a neural property *N*. This is a version of physicalism about human pain: the neural description is taken to concern only physical properties and to express the true nature of human pain in a way that mental descriptions do not. Nevertheless, because human pain and *N* are taken to be numerically identical, it follows that human pain and *N* exist at the same level of nature. That follows by Leibniz's Law: if $x = y$, then x and y share all properties, including the property of existing at a given level of nature. Now consider a variant of the Lewis/Armstrong view, on which human pain is identified not with *N* but with some basic physical phenomenon, such as *Q*, an instantiation of a quantum property of the type Brown (2023) describes (see Section 3 above). According to this variant of physicalist realizer functionalism, human pain and *Q* are numerically identical. So, because *Q* exists at the most fundamental physical level, so does human pain. Yet the view is compatible with the physicalist claim that mental phenomena are, or are ultimately grounded entirely in, physical phenomena.

Reductionist physicalism. All of that suggests that the NFM constraint should be understood as the primitive-mentality-based version rather than the levels-based version. That conclusion can be further supported by considering a complication about levels-based fundamentality regarding what is supposed to exist at the most fundamental level.[15] Consider a version of reductionist physicalism on which ordinary macroscopic entities, such as tables, are numerically identical with microphysical phenomena that compose them—phenomena that, let us suppose, exist at the most fundamental level. On this view, tables exist on the most fundamental level, in virtue of being numerically identical with relevant microphysical phenomena.[16] Proponents of that view might want to say the same thing about mental phenomena. That is, they might want to say that mental phenomena are numerically identical to microphysical phenomena that exist at the most fundamental level. In that case, mental phenomena would exist on that level, just as tables would. If physicalism entailed the levels-based NFM constraint, then reductionist physicalism of that sort would not qualify as a version of physicalism. That result is implausible. No such implausible result would follow on the primitive-mentality-based interpretation.

[15] Here I thank an anonymous referee for *The Philosophical Quarterly*.

[16] Although reductionist physicalists might maintain such an identity thesis, they need not. The view Chalmers calls type-A materialism is a version of reductionist physicalism, and not all type-A materialists are identity theorists.

Panpsychism. Consider an exchange between Wilson and Stoljar over whether physicalism is compatible with panpsychism. Panpsychism is the view that "mental properties pervade all aspects of the world" (Montero 1999, p. 185). Stoljar writes,

> ... panpsychism per se is not inconsistent with physicalism (cf. Lewis 1983). After all, the fact that there are *some* conscious beings is not contrary to physicalism—why then should the possibility that *everything* is a conscious being be contrary to physicalism? (Stoljar 2022, sec. 4.4; italics in original)

Wilson (2006, pp. 77–79) takes the opposite position. According to her, the possibility that everything is a conscious being *is* contrary to physicalism. The reason, she suggests, is that if everything is a conscious being, then some fundamental beings would be conscious; and physicalism cannot accommodate conscious fundamental beings.

That dispute might seem hard to resolve. On the one hand, Wilson's response to Stoljar's argument is dialectically suspicious. Declaring that, according to physicalism, fundamental beings cannot be conscious comes perilously close to assuming her conclusion, that physicalism and panpsychism conflict. On the other hand, there is at least a prima facie tension between physicalism and panpsychism, and it is plausible that this tension derives partly from the specter of fundamental mentality, with which panpsychism is associated.

The apparent difficulty in resolving the Wilson–Stoljar dispute can be traced to the ambiguity I have been emphasizing. If we understand "fundamental mentality" in the levels-based sense, then Stoljar's position is the more reasonable one. Physicalism-friendly mentality might reside at any level of reality, including the most fundamental level. But if we understand "fundamental mentality" in the primitive-mentality-based sense, then Wilson's position is the more reasonable one. Primitive mentality is not physicalism friendly (because it is neither identical to nor grounded in physical* phenomena). Neither is quasi-primitive mentality. If panpsychism entails the existence of either, which it well might (Strawson 2006), then Wilson is right: panpsychism is inconsistent with physicalism.[17]

[17] Baltimore (2013) defends a position akin to Stoljar's (2022). According to Baltimore, the NFM constraint wrongly entails that physicalism rules out panpsychism. The points I make about Stoljar's argument apply to Baltimore's, *mutatis mutandis.*

Thus, the distinction between levels-based and primitive-mentality-based fundamental mentality provides a way to resolve the Stoljar–Wilson dispute. But that is not my main reason for mentioning that dispute. My main reason is that the resolution reinforces the conclusion that the primitive-mentality-based NFM constraint is plausible whereas the levels-based version is not. If that conclusion is true, then the principle of charity entails that, other things being equal, the NFM constraint should be interpreted as the primitive-mentality-based version rather than the levels-based version.

Bottomless worlds. The last point I will make in favor of the primitive-mentality-based interpretation of the NFM constraint concerns worlds without a fundamental level, such as worlds in which everything is infinitely decomposable. Plausibly, physicalism could be true of certain infinitely decomposable worlds. Further, Schaffer (2003) argues that the actual world might be such a world. What should NFM-constraint proponents say about this? If one understands the NFM constraint in the levels-based way, then it will need to be amended to account for this possibility. But how to do that is unclear. Let me explain.

Montero (2006) has made an influential proposal on this score, which I have elsewhere called "the No Low-Level Mentality constraint" (Alter 2022). It says that physicalism is incompatible with the existence of not only fundamental mentality but also an infinite descent of mentality: a chain of decomposition in which mentality appears not just at relatively high (that is, non-fundamental) levels but also at lower levels, at even lower levels, and so on *ad infinitum*. Others endorse versions of that solution (Brown and Ladyman 2009; Schaffer 2017). However, there is a problem: Brown (2017a) has devised a compelling argument against the No Low-Level Mentality constraint.

Brown (2017a, p. 1345) imagines an "all-mental and all-physical world—MPW for short." MPW contains only "a single highest-level system": a brain he calls "Alex." Alex "has parts that are dynamically arranged in such a way that they produce mentality for the thing they compose" (Brown 2017a, p. 1345). The same is true of Alex's parts:

> Alex is made of many interacting components, call them Bretts. Collectively all the Bretts, through their interactions, generate Alex's mentality. But also each Brett is mental, for the same reason Alex is. . . . every entity has high compositional complexity—every Brett has many parts,

> call them Charlies, which cause the Brett[s] to be mental in virtue of the Charlies' interactions. And the same story goes for each Charlie which is composed of little Devins, and so on *infinitely*. (Brown 2017a, p. 1346; italics in original)

In MPW, there is no maximally fundamental level of nature, and mentality appears at every level. There is an infinite descent of mentality. Even so, all that mentality could be physicalism friendly. After all, MPW contains only brains: "brains all the way down" (Brown 2017a, p. 1347). Physicalism could be true of MPW, contrary to what Montero's No Low-Level Mentality constraint implies.

However, notice that Brown's argument depends on a levels-based conception of fundamentality, where for x to be more fundamental than y is for x to exist at a lower level than y in a hierarchy of levels. Therein lies the solution. The key is to recognize that the NFM constraint concerns primitive-mentality-based fundamental mentality, not levels-based fundamental mentality. So understood, the constraint applies to infinitely decomposable worlds such as MPW no less than to worlds that have a maximally fundamental level. And thus, contrary to what Montero et al. assume, there is no need to modify the NFM constraint to account for worlds such as MPW. Although MPW contains an infinite descent of mentality, none of that mentality need be primitively or quasi-primitively mental. Within each level, the mental might still be physically grounded. This helps explain why physicalism could be true of that world.[18] Thus, another advantage of conceiving of the NFM constraint in terms of primitive and quasi-primitive mentality rather than in terms of levels is that doing so avoids a problem of how to extend the constraint to worlds such as MPW.

Although the preceding arguments focus on physicalism, parallel reasoning applies to all versions of monism. That in turn has a notable implication for MT, the monist thesismonist thesis that I discussed in Chapter 1, Section 1. MT says that all actual, concrete phenomena are such that there is exactly one unified, substantive, fundamental nature that they share. What should now be clear is that here "fundamental" need not have any implications for levels of nature. Instead, the idea is that the nature in question is primitive.

[18] For a related solution, see Alter (2022). Alter, Howell, and Coleman (2022) develop a different solution. But see Werner (2025), whose criticism of the Alter–Howell–Coleman solution does not apply to the one I propose here.

5. The counterexamples revisited

The cases devised by Dorsey, Zhong, and Brown might well undermine the levels-based NFM constraint. Though significant, that result does not settle whether those cases undermine the primitive-mentality-based NFM constraint. In this section, I will argue that they do not.

I will begin with Dorsey's case, in which you discover a physical simple and God tells you that it has a mental property. To undermine the primitive-mentality-based NFM constraint, that mental property would have to be primitively mental or quasi-primitively mental. But Dorsey provides no reason to think that the physical simple's mental property is either. Maybe that property qualifies as mental for some other, physicalism-friendly reason. For example, perhaps it plays a relevant functional role in a physically realized cognitive system. If the scenario Dorsey describes involves nothing that is primitively or quasi-primitively mental, then the primitive-mentality-based NFM constraint is not threatened.

Does the fact that what you discover is *simple* constitute a reason to think that its mental property is primitively mental? No, it does not. Presumably, it is the bearer of the mental property that is simple, rather than the mental property itself. Recall that Dorsey (2011, p. 219) describes the simple as "a physical entity with no proper parts." That the entity has no proper parts is not a reason to suppose that it is primitively mental. After all, the "corpuscles" that the early modern philosophers (Descartes, Boyle et al.) described were not thought to have any mental features, let alone primitively mental features. And if having no proper parts were a reason to suppose the entity you discover is primitively mental, then why should we think the scenario is physicalism friendly? Plausibly, in that case, we should not.

Dorsey might respond by adding a further stipulation: God tells you that the physical simple has a property that is not only mental but primitively mental. But that would not help his argument, if he means to challenge the primitive-mentality-based NFM constraint. Given that what God tells you is true, that further stipulation would entail that the physical simple's mental property is not clearly physicalism friendly. In other words, the further stipulation would undermine the basis of Dorsey's claim that the scenario he imagines is compatible with physicalism.

In both of Zhong's cases, a fundamental physical phenomenon turns out to be identical to a mental phenomenon. In one case, S-neutrino fluctuation is both fundamental and identical to consciousness. In another, C-fiber firing turns out to be fundamental and identical to pain. These cases threaten the levels-based NFM constraint. But do they threaten the primitive-mentality-based version? This depends on whether they involve physicalism-friendly phenomena that are primitively or quasi-primitively mental. Do they?

Take S-neutrino fluctuation. This is a mental phenomenon: it is the phenomenon of consciousness. But now we can ask: is this phenomenon grounded in something else, or is it not? Suppose first that it is not grounded in something else. In that case, it is a form of primitive mentality. Therefore, its existence is not compatible with physicalism, on the primitive-mentality-based NFM constraint. The same conclusion follows if S-neutrino fluctuation is quasi-primitively mental. Now suppose S-neutrino fluctuation is grounded in something else, but not ultimately in mentality. In that case, why is S-neutrino fluctuation identical with consciousness? Perhaps it is identical with consciousness in virtue of realizing some physicalism-friendly functional feature. If so, then physicalism might be true: consciousness would be grounded in the physical. But then S-neutrino fluctuation is neither primitively nor quasi-primitively mental. Thus, if S-neutrino fluctuation is grounded in something else or if it is not, the primitive-mentality-based NFM constraint is not threatened. The same point applies, *mutatis mutandis*, to Zhong's C-fiber stimulation case.

Let me turn to Brown's cases, starting with the "more troubling" one, involving an artificially intelligent quantum computer that employs quantum properties as part of its cognitive operations. In Brown's view, one such quantum property might be fundamental, mental, and physicalism friendly: fundamental because it exists at the most fundamental level of nature; mental because it plays an appropriate functional role in the system's mental life; and physicalism friendly because it consists entirely in the obtaining of relations between physicalism-friendly phenomena.

Suppose Brown is right on all three counts. Still, his case does not refute the NFM constraint unless the constraint concerns levels-based fundamental mentality. If instead the constraint concerns the primitive-mentality-based variety, then the threat disappears, because there is no reason to think the case involves primitive or quasi-primitive mentality. If the relevant quantum property of the AI is mental, then it is mental in virtue of its playing a certain functional role. There is no reason to think its mentality is primitive or quasi-primitive—just as there is no reason to think that, on the Lewis/Armstrong view, neural states with which human mental states are identified are primitively mental or quasi-primitively mental.

In response, Brown might argue as follows:

> Let *r* be the quantum property that plays the relevant functional role in the AI's cognitive system ("*r*" for "role-player" or "realizer"). By realizer functionalism, *r* is identical to a mental property *m*. And since *m* is mental, it follows by Leibniz's Law that *r* is mental too. But *r* is fundamental. Thus, *r* is primitively mental.[19]

That response is unconvincing. The quantum property *r* may be fundamentally mental in the levels-based sense. It does not follow that *r* is primitively or quasi-primitively mental. Is there any other reason to conclude that *r* is primitively or quasi-primitively mental? I see none. If *r* is mental, then it is mental in virtue of its playing an appropriate functional role in the AI's cognitive system. That does not entail the existence of primitive or quasi-primitive mentality. Indeed, *r*'s being mental (if it is) is incidental to its playing the relevant functional role. Something non-mental could as easily have done so. For comparison, imagine a drawing of little circular dots arranged in a big circle. The big figure is circular in virtue of the arrangement of the dots. But the dots themselves being circular is irrelevant to their forming that arrangement. They could just as easily have been little squares.[20]

Brown's priority-monism case has the same limitation as his quantum-AI case. Recall that in the priority-monist world he describes, there is only a single brain whose properties "are properties of the whole of nature." To refute the primitive-mentality-based NFM constraint, he would have to show that the brain that he imagines has a physicalism-friendly property that is primitively or quasi-primitively mental, and not merely a physicalism-friendly mental property that exists at the most fundamental level. But he provides no clear reason to think this can be done.

6. Dorsey's distinction

Like me, Dorsey draws a distinction between two kinds of fundamental mentality. He writes:

> **Fundamental mentality (1) = Mentality *that is* fundamental** either mental substances/objects are ontologically fundamental (*meaning they are not*

[19] Zhong and Dorsey could give versions of the same objection. My reply is the same, *mutatis mutandis*.

[20] The circle example is adapted from Alter, Howell, and Coleman (2024).

> *themselves identical to, metaphysically supervenient on, reducible to, etc., physical substances/objects*); or mental properties are ontologically fundamental (*meaning they are not themselves physical properties or identical to, metaphysically supervenient on, etc., physical properties*).... **Fundamental mentality (2) = Mentality *that is instantiated by* a fundamental physical entity** i.e., something is a fundamental physical entity and it instantiates at least one mental property. (Dorsey 2011, p. 216; boldface and italics in original)

Dorsey's distinction corresponds roughly to my distinction between levels-based and primitive-mentality-based fundamental mentality. Fundamental mentality (1) corresponds roughly to primitive-mentality-based fundamental mentality, and fundamental mentality (2) corresponds roughly to levels-based fundamental mentality. Dorsey and I also take similar positions regarding how the distinction bears on physicalism. Just as I hold that physicalism is compatible with the existence of levels-based fundamental mentality, he holds that physicalism is compatible with the existence of fundamental mentality (2). And just as I hold that physicalism is incompatible with the existence of primitive-mentality-based fundamental mentality, he holds that physicalism is incompatible with the existence of fundamental mentality (1).

Nevertheless, Dorsey and I disagree about Wilson's NFM constraint: he rejects it, and I accept it. But it is not clear how deep this disagreement is. He rejects the constraint because he takes it to concern fundamental mentality (2). But he could instead take the constraint to concern fundamental mentality (1). If he did, then he would accept it.

Although my distinction and Dorsey's are similar, they are not identical. In particular, fundamental mentality (1) and primitive-mentality-based fundamental mentality are not equivalent. The existence of the former does not entail the existence of the latter. To see this, consider the neutral properties posited by neutral monism. Such properties would (or at least could) satisfy Dorsey's description of fundamental mentality (1): they are not identical to, metaphysically supervenient on, etc., physical properties. But neutral properties are neither primitively mental nor quasi-primitively mental: they are primitively neutral. So, fundamental mentality (1) might exist even if primitive-mentality-based fundamental mentality does not.

What about the reverse entailment? Does the existence of primitive-mentality-based fundamental mentality entail the existence of fundamental mentality (1)? This too seems doubtful. Consider an idealist version of the identity theory on which physical properties are identical to primitively mental properties. This version inverts the familiar physicalist version, on which the physical properties with which mental properties are identified have metaphysical priority. For example, whereas on the familiar identity theory, pain is really just C-fiber stimulation (or some other physical phenomenon), on the idealist version of the theory, C-fiber stimulation is really just pain. Suppose the idealist version is true. In that case, it might be that all "mental substances/objects" are primitively mental but nonetheless "themselves identical to . . . physical substances/objects." That is, it might be that primitive-mentality-based fundamental mentality exists but fundamental mentality (1) does not.

7. Conclusion

I began this chapter by presenting a third argument for the monism-matters thesis: that physicalism, idealism, and neutral monism are versions of monism helps explain why those theories entail repudiation theses, such as the physicalist's repudiation of fundamental mentality—a repudiation thesis expressed by Wilson's NFM constraint. I then considered a challenge to her constraint: coherent cases in which, it is alleged, physicalism could be true despite the existence of fundamental mentality. In response, I distinguished between two sorts of fundamental mentality: levels-based and primitive-mentality-based. The alleged counterexamples all assume that the NFM constraint concerns the levels-based sort. I argued that the NFM constraint should instead be understood as concerning the primitive-mentality-based sort, and I showed how this defangs the alleged counterexamples. Along the way, I noted that in MT the term "fundamental" should be understood as concerning the relevant nature's being primitive rather than as concerning levels of nature. Finally, I compared the distinction between levels-based fundamental mentality and primitive-mentality-based fundamental mentality with a similar distinction that Dorsey draws. I suggested that his distinction positions him to accept a version of the NFM constraint that is similar to the one I defend.

6
Three More Arguments for the Significance of Monism

In this chapter, I will present three more arguments for the monism-matters thesis. Each turns on the idea that considerations about monism help determine an issue that has significance for the mind-body debate, thereby figuring importantly in that debate.[1] The relevant issues are as follows: whether the physical can be defined negatively, as the not-fundamentally-mental; whether the physical can be defined deferentially, in terms of what physics posits; and whether the question of the compatibility of physicalism and the existence of fundamental mentality is merely verbal. Based partly on considerations about monism, I will argue that the physical should be defined neither negatively nor deferentially and that the question of how to define the physical is not merely verbal. Further, I will argue, each of these results constitutes a reason to accept the monism-matters thesis.

1. *Via negativa* physicalism

According to *via negativa* physicalism (Spurrett and Papineau 1999, Levine 2001, Montero 2005, Montero and Papineau 2005, Worley 2006, Fiorese 2016), the physical is defined negatively, as the not-fundamentally-mental (or something along similar lines). On such a definition, physicalism requires that all phenomena lack fundamentally mental features but not that there is any positive feature that all phenomena share. In this section, I will argue that if physicalism is a version of monism, then the *via negativa* definition of physicalism is inadequate. If sound, that argument will provide further support for the monism-matters thesis.

[1] When I say that certain considerations *help determine* a significant mind-body debate issue, I mean that to entail that those considerations *figure importantly* in that debate in the sense I described in Chapter 1, Section 4.

Monism Matters. Torin Alter, Oxford University Press.
DOI: 10.1093/9780198931560.003.0007

Via negativa physicalism is often presented as a semantic view, which says that "physical" means "not fundamentally mental" (or something similar). *Via negativa* physicalism can also be seen as a metaphysical view, which says that being physical consists entirely in not being fundamentally mental. For present purposes, either of those formulations will suffice. But both should be distinguished from two views in the vicinity. One is a methodological view, according to which it is useful to conceive of the physical as the not-fundamentally-mental, but the meaning of "physical" is left open (Spurrett 2001, Witmer 2018). The other is an epistemic view, according to which we do not know of any unified, substantive feature in which being physical consists, though such a feature might exist unbeknownst to us. The latter, epistemic view might provide motivation for the former, methodological view. In any case, neither of those views need concern us here.

The main problem I wish to raise for *via negativa* physicalism is this. Suppose physicalism is a version of monism. It follows that if physicalism is true, then there is a unified, substantive, fundamental, physical nature that all actual, concrete phenomena share. But there is no such nature if, as *via negativa* physicalism says, what it is to be physical is just to be not fundamentally mental. On that view, the only relevant universally shared feature is an absence: all phenomena lack fundamental mentality. But that is not sufficient for their sharing a unified, substantive nature any more than their being distinct from the number 37 is.[2]

Another monism-related problem for *via negativa* physicalism concerns neutral monism. On neutral monism, there is no fundamental mentality: mentality is a manifestation of a deeper reality, which is neither physical nor mental and thus not fundamentally mental. Therefore, on the *via negativa* definition of the physical, neutral properties qualify as physical. Neutral monism would then be counted as a version of physicalism. That result is implausible. Physicalists and neutral monists disagree on the relative metaphysical priority of the mental and the physical. Physicalists take the physical to have metaphysical priority over the mental. Although neutral monists might adopt that stance, they need not. Typically, neutral monists take the mental and the physical to be metaphysically on a par. In their view, both are underlain by the neutral. That is a consequence of neutral monism's

[2] Cf. Stoljar (2010, pp. 87–88). Why do *not being fundamentally mental* or *not being the number 37* fail to qualify as a unified, substantive nature? Here I will not attempt to answer that question. But see Bowyer (n.d.), who (following Zangwill 2011) suggests a plausible answer: no negative properties are fundamental.

being a version of monism that specifies the one fundamental nature that everything shares as neutral. Thus, the *via negativa* definition of the physical is overly broad.

The foregoing considerations suggest the following argument for the monism-matters thesis. Considerations about monism help determine a significant issue in the mind-body debate: whether *via negativa* physicalism is tenable. Such considerations thereby figure importantly in that debate, and so monism-matters thesis is true. In standard form:

The *Via Negativa* Argument

1. Considerations about monism help determine whether *via negativa* physicalism is tenable.
2. *Via negativa* physicalism plays a significant role in the contemporary mind-body debate.
3. If (i) considerations about monism help determine whether *via negativa* physicalism is tenable and (ii) *via negativa* physicalism plays a significant role in the contemporary mind-body debate, then the monism-matters thesis is true.
4. Therefore, the monism-matters thesis is true.

That argument is valid. Is it sound? I think so. Premise 1 is plausible. If the arguments I adduced against *via negativa* physicalism are cogent, then premise 1 is justified. Those arguments might not be cogent. Even so, arguably they significantly advance the discussion of whether *via negativa* physicalism is tenable. That would also justify premise 1. Premise 2 is plausible too. *Via negativa* physicalism is a contender view, which is taken seriously by prominent contributors to the contemporary literature, including Levine (2001), Montero (2005), and David Papineau (Montero and Papineau 2005), among others. And premise 3 is true by definition.[3]

2. Deferring to physics

In the last section, I raised monism-related problems for defining the physical negatively, as the not-fundamentally-mental. In this section, I will challenge the proposal that the physical should be defined deferentially, in terms

[3] See Chapter 1, Section 4.

of the posits of physics. I will raise three problems for that proposal, two of which involve monism in a significant way.

Before I begin, I will note two preliminaries. First, the proposal in question leaves open which physical theory the definition concerns: current physical theory or ideal physical theory. I will focus on the latter option. But my criticisms apply equally to the former, *mutatis mutandis*. Second, I will assume that the deferential definition in question concerns only the most fundamental physical phenomena, that is, physical* phenomena.[4] Physicalists might want to count macroscopic objects such as rocks as physical, even if it is unlikely that ideal physics will posit rocks (Stroud 2000, ch. 3). But arguably on all versions of physicalism, rocks are at least grounded in physical* phenomena (Chalmers 2004). So, the question of how the physical is defined can be seen as determined (in part) by how the physical* is defined.

The main problem with defining the physical* deferentially is that this approach seems to get the order of explanation backwards. Take a certain putatively physical* phenomenon P that ideal physics posits. Is P physical* because it is posited by ideal physics? Or is P posited by ideal physics because it is physical*, by some independent criterion of physicality*? The latter answer seems more plausible, at least given the assumption that physicalism is a version of monism. *Being a posit of ideal physics* does not seem to have the sort of unity that MT calls for.

Here my gripe is not with the biconditional: x is physical* if and only if x is posited by ideal physics.[5] What concerns me is rather the idea that the order of explanation goes right to left, that is, that he reason x qualifies as physical* is that x is posited by ideal physics. I claim that the reverse explanation is intuitively the more plausible one: the reason x is posited by ideal physics is that x is physical*, where what it means to be physical* is determined independently. I am not alone in having that attitude. Howell writes,

> There is a sort of "Euthyphro" question here: "Are physical things physical because physics studies them, or does physics study them because they have certain features?" If the former was the case, what reason would a physicist have to add something (or eliminate something) from his field of

[4] Nevertheless, I will sometimes continue to omit the asterisk where it is clear from the context that the relevant physical phenomena are the most fundamental sort.

[5] I accept that biconditional, provided that ideal physics posits only structural phenomena, in a sense of "structural" that I will discuss in Chapter 8, Section 5.

> study? The posits of physics would seem to have an air of arbitrariness. If the latter, and there is some feature that makes things the appropriate study of physics, then that looks to be the sort of feature that should figure into a definition of physicalism. (Howell 2013, p. 16)[6]

Another problem with defining the physical* deferentially relates to an issue discussed in Chapter 5, Section 4. Defining the physical* deferentially might require invoking Wilson's NFM (No Fundamental Mentality) constraint to ensure that fundamental mentality does not qualify as a basic ingredient of the physical world. But as monists, physicalists repudiate not only fundamental mental phenomena but also fundamentally neutral phenomena. Therefore, defining the physical* deferentially seems to require invoking not only an NFM constraint but also a No Fundamental Neutrality constraint.

It does not end there. Wilson and others focus on fundamental mentality because the contemporary debate largely centers on whether certain sorts of mental phenomena, such as consciousness, can be accommodated within a physicalist framework. But this has not always been the case. In the nineteenth and early twentieth centuries, there was a prominent debate about whether physicalism (or materialism, as it was then more often called) can accommodate certain truths about *living* phenomena, that is, whether nature includes a non-physical *élan vital* (life force).[7] Wilson might therefore need to add a No Fundamental Vitality constraint too. Indeed, she might need to add yet more such constraints: one for every fundamental type of phenomenon the existence of which physicalists repudiate. Another example might be a No Fundamental Normativity constraint (FitzPatrick 2022).

Here one might object that the chances of ideal physics positing vitality or normativity are extremely low. But a definition of the physical should not leave this matter up to chance. So, it appears that the deferential approach requires adding several constraints similar to Wilson's NFM constraint. Doing so can seem implausibly ad hoc. Arguably, any deferential definition of the physical will have this problem.

A third problem for defining the physical deferentially concerns non-actual possible worlds. Other things being equal, it would be preferable

[6] Although in this passage Howell uses "physical" rather than "physical*," he has physical* properties in mind. See Howell (2013, pp. 16, 41).

[7] Fiorese (2016) argues that the challenge concerning an irreducible life force turns on considerations about mentality. But see Stojar (2022).

for a definition of the physical to apply not just to actual phenomena but to merely possible phenomena as well. And is not clear how to achieve that goal, if the physical is defined by reference to physics. Arguably, there might have been physical phenomena that are neither posited by physics—even ideal physics—nor grounded in phenomena it posits. After all, the phenomena physics aims to explain are all actual. How should this be addressed?

Wilson intends her "physics-based NFM account" of the physical to apply across possible worlds. Here is her formulation:

> *The physics-based NFM account*: An entity existing at a world *w* is physical if and only if
> (i)′ It is treated, approximately accurately, by current or future (in the limit of inquiry, ideal) versions of fundamental physics at *w*, and
> (ii) It is not fundamentally mental (that is, does not individually either possess or bestow mentality)
> It is assumed here that anything that counts as physics at a world will share with actual physics the features of being a science treating of the relatively fundamental entities. (Wilson 2006, p. 72; italics in original)[8]

On Wilson's physics-based NFM account, an object *o* is physical at possible world *w* only if *o* is "treated . . . by physics at *w*." Presumably, "physics at *w*" refers to a science conducted by intelligent creatures who exist in *w*. Suppose that, at non-actual world w_1, there are no intelligent creatures, and thus there is no science, but there are electrons. Electrons would not be treated by the physics at w_1, simply because there is no physics at w_1. Thus, Wilson's account seems to entail that those electrons are not physical. That verdict seems implausible. Intuitively, they might be physical (Alter 2023, p. 215, fn. 25).

It might be possible to address that problem by modifying Wilson's account. But how to do so is not clear. It will not suffice to add a clause such as "or at the actual world" after "at *w*" at the end of clause (i′), so that (i′) says "it is treated . . . by current or future (in the limit of inquiry, ideal) versions of

[8] Wilson (2006, p. 93, fn. 4) qualifies "fundamental" with "relatively" for two reasons: "First, many entities treated by physics are not themselves fundamental—e.g., protons. Second, notwithstanding physicalism's foundationalist aspirations, satisfying these aspirations does not entail a commitment to their being a fundamental level." Regarding the latter reason, see Chapter 5, Section 4.

fundamental physics at *w or at the actual world*." To see why that will not suffice, suppose w_1 contains not only electrons but also alien phenomena, that is, phenomena of a sort that the actual world does not contain. Intuitively, such alien phenomena might be physical. They would not be treated by physics at w_1 if there is no physics at w_1. Nor would they be treated at the actual world, because they do not exist here. So, even with the proposed modification of clause (i′), Wilson's account would appear to be overly narrow.

What if instead we added the following to the end of clause (i′): "or would be treated by physics at *w* if there is such a science at *w*"? Would that solve the narrowness problem for Wilson's account? Perhaps. But that would raise the question of why a given phenomenon *x* would be treated by a merely possible physics at *w* (or if *x* would not be so treated at *w*, why it would not). In response, Wilson might say that *x* would be treated by that science if and only if *x* is fundamental but not fundamentally mental. But then it is not clear what clause (i′) adds to clause (ii). Also, what if *x* is fundamentally neutral?

Like Wilson and many others, Alyssa Ney (2008) favors a deferential approach to defining the physical. But Ney takes deference to physics a step further. In her view, not only should we defer to physics when it comes to defining the physical, we should regard physicalism itself as a kind of deferential attitude. Physicalism, she proposes, is not committed to a thesis that is true or false. Instead, "Physicalism is an attitude one takes to form one's ontology completely and solely according to what physics says exists" (Ney 2008, p. 9). That attitude can be expressed as an oath such as the following:

> (PC) I hereby swear to go in my ontology everywhere and only where physics leads me. (Ney 2008, p. 5)[9]

Taking physicalism to be merely an attitude represents a substantial departure from the mainstream. According to Ney, doing so is justified because it allows us to avoid Hempel's dilemma.[10] She points out that Hempel's dilemma concerns theses that are "truth-evaluable" (Ney 2008, p. 3), such as the claim that current physics posits all basic physical phenomena—a claim

[9] "PC" might abbreviate "physicalist commitment"; Ney does not say. She describes PC as "only one of a family of different oaths that might properly be described as 'physicalist'" (Ney 2008, p. 11). Another member of that family is: "(PC′) I hereby swear to believe in the existence of all and only those entities posited by current physics and those entities composed of the entities of current physics."

[10] See Chapter 2, Section 4 and Chapter 5, Section 2

that is probably false. By contrast, oaths such as PC are not truth evaluable. Ney writes,

> This view has the virtue of avoiding both horns of Hempel's dilemma. . . .it avoids both horns since by giving up status as a doctrine, the view cannot be false or trivial; attitudes are not properly evaluable as true, false, or trivial. (Ney 2008, p. 10)

Ney's view is intriguing. But it conflicts with the claim that physicalism is a version of monism, at least given how I have explicated monism. On that explication, any version of monism is, at least in part, a truth-evaluable thesis.[11] Further, the principal argument Ney offers for her view is questionable. Hempel's dilemma is usually stated in such a way that it applies only to versions of physicalism that are truth evaluable. But one might argue that attitudinal physicalism runs into an analogous dilemma. Let me explain.

Even if we cannot evaluate oaths and attitudes as true or false, we can evaluate them along other dimensions. For example, we can evaluate oaths as rational or not, and as less or more rational.[12] Perhaps it is rational to follow physics where and only where it leads, or perhaps doing so is more rational than an alternative attitude, such as one associated with a non-physicalist theory such as dualism. But to what does "physics" refer—current physical theory or ideal physical theory? There would seem to be problems either way.

Should the theory we follow be current physical theory? That is what Ney (2008, p. 10) suggests. But because current physical theory is incomplete, following it only where it leads might have us fail to include something in our ontology simply because it has yet to be discovered. Further, current theory is likely not fully accurate. So, following it where it leads might have us include something in our ontology that does not actually exist. Those consequences need not make it irrational to follow current physical theory where and only where it leads. But they seem to indicate that doing so is less rational than following ideal physical theory instead. Yet doing that might result in our positing fundamental mentality of a sort that is not compatible with physicalism. Whichever route we choose, our attitude does not seem optimally rational,

[11] The same point applies to proposals similar to Ney's, for example, that physicalism should be regarded not as a truth-evaluable thesis but rather as a methodological position (Poland 2003) or a research program (Elpidorou and Dove 2018).

[12] Ney (2008, p. 12) implies as much, when she observes that it would be "fair to criticize" the attitudinal physicalist for endorsing PC, should it turn out that physics posits "irreducible mental entities."

from a physicalist viewpoint. Thus, trading ontological physicalism for attitudinal physicalism might not have the advantage that Ney claims it has.

None of the problems I have raised for defining the physical deferentially need arise for non-deferential definitions. First, a non-deferential definition could affirm the intuitive left-to-right order of explanation with respect to the biconditional: *x* is physical* if and only if *x* is posited by ideal physics. For example, suppose we accept the truth of that biconditional. Suppose also that we accept neocart as a complete and exclusive definition of the physical* (again, neocart says that a property is physical* if and only if its nature can be fully characterized in terms of its spatiotemporal implications). Finally, for purposes of illustration, suppose that quarks satisfy neocart. It follows that quarks both qualify as physical* and are posited by ideal physics. Now consider two competing claims: (i) quarks are physical* because they are posited by ideal physics; and (ii) quarks are posited by ideal physics because they are physical*. It is hard to see how we could affirm (i). To do so would be to imply that neocart does not define the physical*, at least not completely and exclusively, contrary to our supposition. By contrast, we could affirm (ii). Indeed, it is hard to see how we could not.

Second, defining the physical non-deferentially might help explain why physicalists repudiate fundamental mentality, fundamental neutrality, etc., in a way that is not ad hoc. For example, arguably by neocart fundamentally mental phenomena, fundamentally neutral phenomena, etc., will not qualify as physical on the grounds that their natures would not be exhausted by their spatiotemporal implications—assuming spacetime itself is not fundamentally mental, fundamentally normative, etc.[13] Finally, a non-deferential definition could apply straightforwardly to merely possible phenomena. For example, recall non-actual world w_1, which contains electrons but no intelligent creatures. Neocart could classify the electrons at w_1 as physical for the same reasons it could so classify actual electrons: an electron at w_1 would qualify if and only if its nature is exhausted by its spatiotemporal implications. Similar reasoning applies to alien phenomena: they qualify as physical if and only if their natures are exhausted by their spatiotemporal implications.

All of this calls for revisiting the motivation for defining the physical deferentially, in terms of the posits of ideal physics. As I noted in Chapter 2, Section 5, the main motivation is to avoid past errors.[14] For example, defining the physical in terms of three-dimensional extension turned out to be inadequate because

[13] That assumption might be questioned. See Chapter 8, Sections 4 and 5.

[14] Historically, the deferential approach is also connected to logical positivism. See Chapter 1, Section 5 and Chapter 2, Section 5.

of developments in modern physics. As I also noted in Chapter 2, Section 5, although we should be mindful of that sort of danger, we should not exaggerate it. Granted, we should be careful not to marry our conception of the physical to aspects of current physics that might well not be part of ideal physics. Also, any such conception should be informed by careful reflection on the sorts of phenomena physics posits. But as Howell (2012, 2013, ch. 1) argues, it is premature to conclude that no non-deferential definition of the physical can avoid the problems that beset those formed in the seventeenth century.

The claim that physicalism is a version of monism figures significantly into some of the problems I have raised for defining the physical deferentially. This suggests another argument for the monism-matters thesis:

The Argument Concerning Deferential Definitions

1. Considerations about monism help determine whether deferential definitions of the physical are tenable.
2. Deferential definitions of the physical play a significant role in the contemporary mind-body debate.
3. If (i) considerations about monism help determine whether deferential definitions of the physical are tenable and (ii) such definitions play a significant role in the contemporary mind-body debate, then the monism-matters thesis is true.
4. Therefore, the monism-matters thesis is true.

That argument is valid. Is it sound? I think so. Premise 1 is plausible. If the arguments I adduced against defining the physical deferentially are cogent, then premise 1 is justified. Those arguments might not be cogent. Even so, arguably they significantly advance the discussion of whether such a deferential definition is tenable. That would also justify premise 1. Premise 2 is plausible too. Indeed, that the physical should be defined deferentially could reasonably be described as the default position in the contemporary literature on the mind–body problem. And premise 3 is true by definition.[15]

3. A verbal dispute?

In Chapter 5, I defended Wilson's view that physicalism is incompatible with the existence of fundamental mentality (in the primitive-mentality sense).

[15] See Chapter 1, Section 4.

Chalmers (2011) argues that this compatibility issue has verbal elements. One could read him as implying that the issue is merely verbal and therefore not substantive.[16] In this section, I will challenge that potential implication, based partly on arguments I gave in the preceding section.

Chalmers writes,

> One frequently finds verbal elements in disputes over the formulation of physicalism. For example, some physicalists hold that physicalism is the thesis that everything supervenes on the properties invoked by a completed physics (whether or not they are mental), while others hold that physicalism is the thesis that everything supervenes on the properties invoked by a completed physics and that these properties are non-mental. To adjudicate whether this dispute is verbal, one can bar 'physicalism', introduce 'physicalism$_1$' and 'physicalism$_2$', and see whether there is a residual disagreement.
>
> Here, residual substantive disagreements are not easy to find. The most likely candidates are sociological or normative claims: for example, "Physicalism$_1$ is what people in a certain debate are concerned with," "Physicalism$_1$ is the more important issue," or "Physicalism$_1$ is what matters for purpose *X*." Even in these cases, however, it is not clear that any of these sentences will be such that the subjects disagree about it, and such that resolving that disagreement would resolve the original disagreement. But in any case, if these are the residual disagreements, then one can focus on these issues, putting the debate in the sociological or normative realm where it belongs. (Chalmers 2011, pp. 17–18)[17]

What should we infer from those reflections? Should we infer that the issue of whether physicalism is compatible with the existence of fundamental mentality is merely verbal and therefore not substantive? I think not. Let us follow Chalmers's suggestion for how to adjudicate this matter. Let us stipulate that physicalism$_1$ is "the thesis that everything supervenes on the properties invoked by a completed physics (whether or not they are mental)" and that physicalism$_2$ is "the thesis that everything supervenes on

[16] Chalmers does not assert this, and perhaps he would disavow it. If so, then my criticism should be taken as a reason not to read him as implying that the compatibility issue is merely verbal.

[17] In this passage, Chalmers seems to assume the sort of deferential conception of the physical that I argued against in Section 2. But that assumption seems inessential to his reasoning.

the properties invoked by a completed physics and that these properties are non-mental." Is it true that "residual substantive disagreements are not easy to find"?

No, it is not. Consider one of the allegedly sociological or normative claims that Chalmers lists as the most likely candidates for substantive disagreement: "Physicalism$_1$ is what matters for purpose *X*." Replace "purpose *X*" with "the philosophical debate about fundamental ontology in which monism, dualism, neutral monism, and nihilism compete." That replacement yields the following candidate for substantive disagreement:

> (FO) Physicalism$_1$ is what matters for the philosophical debate about fundamental ontology in which monism, dualism, neutral monism, and nihilism compete.[18]

Presumably, Dorsey, Zhong, and Brown would argue that FO is established by cases they devise, such as Zhong's imagined case of S-neutrino fluctuation being identical to consciousness. By contrast, I take the arguments presented in Chapter 5 to show otherwise. I also take those arguments to imply that it is not physicalism$_1$ but rather physicalism$_2$ (or something along similar lines) that matters for the relevant philosophical debate about fundamental ontology. That residual disagreement between me and Dorsey et al. was easy to find.

What should we make of the suggestion that focusing on that residual disagreement puts it "in the sociological or normative realm where it belongs"? Here I will note two points. First, even if that disagreement belongs in the sociological or normative realm, it does not follow that the disagreement is merely verbal. After all, there are substantive disagreements in both of those realms. Second, it is not clear what exactly the suggestion means. For example, why should the fact that a claim is true or false only relative to some purpose imply that the claim is normative or sociological? Why wouldn't this depend on the purpose (e.g., the claim is sociological if the purpose concerns society)? Perhaps the suggestion means something like the following: physicalism plays a central role in a discussion that has been ongoing for centuries, and debates about physicalism's commitments make sense only relative to that role. The latter claim is plausible. Indeed, arguably it is tacitly accepted

[18] It is not clear to me that FO qualifies as "sociological or normative," except in a very broad sense in which virtually any meta-philosophical claim is sociological or normative. But here this does not matter much.

by all parties to the debate: me, Dorsey et al. If so, then insofar as the residual disagreement between us belongs in the sociological or normative realm, it did not need to be "put" there: it has been there all along.

Chalmers' reflections do not show that whether physicalism is compatible with the existence of fundamental mentality is merely a verbal issue. But they might support a weaker conclusion: that the compatibility issue might appear to be merely verbal if we fail to recognize certain implications of physicalism's being a version of monism, such as those I referenced in Chapter 5 while defending Wilson's NFM constraint against alleged counterexamples. That weaker conclusion suggests another argument for the monism-matters thesis:

The It's-Not-Merely-Verbal Argument

1. Considerations about monism help determine whether the dispute about physicalism's compatibility with fundamental mentality is merely verbal.
2. Whether that dispute is merely verbal is significant to the contemporary mind-body debate.
3. If (i) considerations about monism help determine whether the dispute about physicalism's compatibility with fundamental mentality is merely verbal and (ii) whether that dispute is merely verbal is significant to the contemporary mind-body debate, then the monism-matters thesis is true.
4. Therefore, the monism-matters thesis is true.

That argument is valid. Is it sound? I think so. Premise 1 is plausible. If my criticisms of Chalmers's argument are cogent, then premise 1 is justified. Those criticisms might not be cogent. Even so, arguably they significantly advance the discussion of whether physicalism's compatibility with fundamental mentality is merely verbal. That would also justify premise 1. Premise 2 is plausible too. Whether the dispute about physicalism's compatibility with fundamental mentality is merely verbal has significant implications for the contemporary mind-body debate. For example, if the dispute is merely verbal, then the contributions to it by Dorsey, Zhong, Brown, and me have less significance than one might otherwise suppose. And premise 3 is true by definition.[19]

[19] See Chapter 1, Section 4.

4. Conclusion

In this chapter, I argued that considerations about monism bear importantly on three significant issues in mind-body debate: whether the physical can be defined negatively, as the not-fundamentally-mental; whether the physical can be defined deferentially, in terms of the posits of physics; and whether the question of the compatibility of physicalism and fundamental mentality is merely verbal. Based partly on considerations about monism, I raised problems for defining the physical negatively, for defining the physical deferentially, and for the claim that the question of the compatibility of physicalism and fundamental mentality is merely verbal. Perhaps those problems can be solved or perhaps they cannot. Either way, I suggested, reflecting on them advances the debate. If so, I argued, then that adds further support to the monism-matters thesis.

7
Supervenience Physicalism

In this chapter and the next, I will consider how best to state the physicalist version of monism, that is, the core physicalist thesis to which all standard versions of physicalism are committed.[1] As Lewis remarks, it is easy enough to state that thesis in a rough way. He writes,

> Roughly speaking, Materialism [a.k.a. physicalism] is the thesis that physics—something not too different from present-day physics, though presumably somewhat improved—is a comprehensive theory of the world, complete as well as correct. (Lewis 1983, pp. 33–34).

But as Lewis recognizes, it is harder to state the thesis precisely. I take this to consist in stating a proposition that expresses, in an illuminating way, all and only physicalism's core commitments.

Given what I have already said about physicalism, one way to state that proposition suggests itself: physicalism's core thesis is a special case of MT, where the fundamental nature MT posits is physical. I endorse that proposition. But that leaves at least two issues unresolved. We still lack an adequate characterization of the physical. I will address that issue in Sections 4 and 5 of Chapter 8. We also lack an adequate characterization of how the most basic physical phenomena (that is, physical* phenomena) relate to other phenomena that many physicalists countenance, such as rocks and tables. I will address that issue in the present chapter and in Sections 1–3 of Chapter 8.

Lewis (1983) and Jaegwon Kim (1993) propose characterizing the core physicalist thesis as a supervenience thesis, such as PSV* any world that is a minimal physical* duplicate of our world is a duplicate simpliciter of our world.[2] That proposal is now widely rejected. Most agree that

[1] Whenever I refer to stating physicalism, I mean stating that core thesis. Also, when discussing that issue, I use "state," "characterize," "formulate," and "define" interchangeably.

[2] In this chapter and the next, I sometimes use "supervenience" to refer to a supervenience thesis associated with physicalism, such as PSV*. Neither Lewis nor Kim formulate supervenience as PSV*. But the differences in formulation do not matter much here.

Monism Matters. Torin Alter, Oxford University Press. © Torin Alter 2026.
DOI: 10.1093/9780198931560.003.0008

supervenience is necessary for physicalism, that is, that physicalism is true only if a supervenience thesis such as PSV* is true.[3] But several argue that supervenience is not sufficient for physicalism. In their view, supervenience could hold even if physicalism is false. The latter group includes Horgan (1993), Melnyk (2003, ch. 2), Wilson (2005, 2021), and Witmer (2020), among others.[4] However, the issue remains controversial. Howell (2009, 2013) attacks the anti-sufficiency argument of Horgan et al. and Wilson (2021) defends it against his attack.

In this chapter, I will argue that Howell has the upper hand in his dispute with Wilson. But I will also show how to modify the anti-sufficiency argument he attacks in a way that avoids his criticism. So, I will ultimately agree with Horgan et al., that supervenience is not sufficient for physicalism. That will set the stage for Chapter 8, where I will propose a positive characterization of the central physicalist thesis—a characterization that makes use of metaphysical grounding and a revised version of Howell's neocart.

1. The Argument from Emergentism

Above I quoted Lewis's rough statement of the core physicalist thesis. It will be convenient to consider an even rougher statement: "Everything is physical." We can then conceive of the general problem of how to state physicalism more precisely as comprising three specific problems, which correspond to the three words that statement contains. In Howell's (2013, p. 10) terminology: the *domain* problem concerns how to understand what is included in "Everything," that is, the scope of the thesis; *the base problem* concerns how to understand what counts as "physical," or more precisely, "physical*"; and *the relation problem* concerns how to understand "is," that is, the relationship between the base (physical*) phenomena and other phenomena in the domain.

The proposal that physicalism is a supervenience thesis is meant to address the relation problem, which is the main focus of this chapter. According to

[3] As Montero (2013, p. 93) writes, "most, if not all" of those "engaged in the debate over the mind–body problem . . . agree that if physicalism is true, then mental properties must supervene on fundamental physical properties." But see Chapter 4.

[4] Kim could also be included in this list, despite his earlier (Kim 1993) endorsement of the sufficiency of supervenience for physicalism. See Kim (2005, p. 14). But see also Kim (2011), where he seems revert to his earlier position.

that proposal, the relation between the physical* phenomena in the base and the other phenomena in the domain should be construed as supervenience. Horgan (1993), Melnyk (2003), Wilson (2005, 2021), and others base their rejection of that proposal partly on the alleged consistency of the physicalist's mental-physical supervenience thesis with emergentism. As I use the term here, *emergentism* is a non-physicalist theory on which mental properties are over and above physical properties.[5] According to Horgan et al., it could be that emergentism is true and mental–physical supervenience holds all the same. If so, then mental–physical supervenience is not sufficient for physicalism.

How could emergentism and mental–physical supervenience both be true? Melnyk illustrates that possibility by imagining that, in creating the concrete world, God simply sets things up so that mental–physical supervenience obtains. Wilson (2005, 2021, p. 143) elaborates on that idea. She imagines a version of Malebranchean occasionalism, in which a Malebranchean (1674–5/1980) God makes it the case that, in all possible worlds, certain mental features are instantiated whenever certain lower-level physical features are instantiated. Wilson (2021, p. 143) describes that scenario as "somewhat fanciful but metaphysically coherent." Further, she suggests, that scenario is consistent with emergentism. And she takes that to show that mental–physical supervenience might obtain even if physicalism is false.

To establish that conclusion, Wilson does not rely solely on the Malebranchean scenario. She also appeals to a necessitarian view about natural laws (Shoemaker 1980; Swoyer 1982; Bird 2007). Such natural laws might include laws posited by emergentism: laws governing the emergence of mental features from physical features. Given necessitarianism about natural laws, such emergence laws would obtain with metaphysical necessity. That would guarantee that the mental supervenes on the physical. Once again, it seems to follow that mental–physical supervenience is consistent with (non-physicalist) emergentism and, therefore, does not entail physicalism.

The emergence-based anti-sufficiency argument of Horgan et al. could be summarized in standard form as follows:[6]

[5] It is common to distinguish weak emergentism and strong emergentism, where the former is a version of physicalism, and the latter is not (Wilson 2021). Throughout, by "emergentism" I mean the strong, non-physicalist version.

[6] Here PSV* serves as proxy for the relevant mental-physical supervenience thesis; however, the latter is formulated.

The Argument from Emergentism

1. Emergentism, a non-physicalist theory, is consistent with PSV*.
2. If emergentism is consistent with PSV*, then PSV* is not sufficient for physicalism.[7]
3. Therefore, PSV* is not sufficient for physicalism.

2. Howell's Base Pollution Argument

Howell (2009, 2013) defends supervenience physicalism against the anti-sufficiency argument of Horgan et al. In effect, he rejects premise 1 of The Argument From Emergentism, arguing that emergentism is not consistent with PSV*. He starts with the idea that properties are individuated at least partly by their modally necessary features, that is, the features they metaphysically necessitate. That idea fits uneasily with the combination of emergentism and PSV*. If emergentism is true, then mental properties are non-physical. If PSV* is also true, then physical properties in the supervenience base metaphysically necessitate non-physical properties. What would explain that necessitation? According to Howell, the answer is that the base properties could not be "purely" physical. Instead, they would be "polluted": "infused with mentality" in a way that renders them unfit for "a purely physical supervenience base" (Howell 2013, p. 51). Following Kevin Morris (2014), I will refer to Howell's argument as *The Base Pollution Argument.*

Being infused with mentality need not imply instantiating mental properties. Howell explains why with his own fanciful thought experiment:

> Schmairs are just like chairs, except that when zombies sit in them they are suddenly conscious. . . .Schmairs might not themselves be conscious, but a fundamental, irreducible part of what makes them what they are is the disposition to confer consciousness. . . .If electrons, or the basic constituents of our world, have a similarly brute non-physical disposition, then the basic stuff of our world is . . . infused with mentality in that it is individuated by the brute tendency to produce it. (Howell 2013, pp. 50–51)

[7] By "PSV* is not sufficient for physicalism," I mean: "it is not the case that: if PSV* is true, then physicalism is true."

The flaw Howell sees in The Argument from Emergentism is, then, this. According to PSV*, mental properties supervene on unpolluted (or "pure") physical properties, that is, physical properties that are not infused with mentality in the way that schmairs are. Emergentism is not consistent with that supervenience thesis. Emergentism *is* consistent with an analogous supervenience thesis, where the so-called physical base properties are polluted in the way that schmairs are—but the latter thesis is not equivalent to PSV*.

Regarding necessitarianism about natural laws, Howell writes,

> Even given necessitarianism about laws, emergentism is not a counterexample to [the sufficiency of supervenience for physicalism]. The basic argument is that if emergence laws are necessary, and the emergent properties are "new" enough to count as non-physical, then the supervenience base will be polluted and will no longer be purely physical. If this is the case, then . . . duplicating the purely physical properties will not duplicate the world *simpliciter*. (Howell 2013, p. 49; italics in original)

So, according to Howell, if emergence laws are metaphysically necessary, then the base properties on which emergent, non-physical mental properties supervene are not "purely physical."

Howell considers the scenario Wilson describes, in which God simply makes modal space such that "every world with a physical base came paired with a certain set of non-physical properties" (Howell 2013, p. 52). About that scenario, he writes,

> We can ask the following question about this situation: did God have to make things this way or not? If he didn't have to, then there are other possibilities and thus other possible worlds where there isn't the pairing, and supervenience fails. If God did have to make things this way, why? Presumably for the same reason he cannot make squares without corners—just as corners are part of the nature of squares, certain dualistic states would have to be part of the nature of "physical" states. (Howell 2013, pp. 52–53)

That last point helps clarify an important aspect of Howell's Base Pollution Argument. If the non-physical mental properties in the scenarios Melnyk and Wilson imagine are metaphysically necessitated by the base properties, then this necessitation cannot be brute and unexplained. Rather, it must trace to the nature of those base properties. They would then be polluted: mentally infused, just as schmairs are. It follows that the scenarios Melnyk and Wilson imagine are not genuine counterexamples to the claim that mental–physical supervenience is sufficient for physicalism.

Howell's Base Pollution Argument could be stated in standard form as follows, where "the base properties" refers to the properties in the supervenience base of a mental–physical supervenience thesis:

The Base Pollution Argument

1. Emergentism entails that the base properties either brutely necessitate mental properties or are infused with mentality in a way that renders them non-physical.
2. The base properties do not brutely necessitate mental properties.
3. So, emergentism entails that the base properties are infused with mentality in a way that renders them non-physical.
4. If emergentism entails that the base properties are infused with mentality in a way that renders them non-physical, then The Argument from Emergentism fails.
5. Thus, The Argument from Emergentism fails.

3. Wilson's responses to Howell's argument

So formulated, The Base Pollution argument is valid. Is it sound? I will not attempt to fully resolve that issue. But I will argue that Wilson's (2021) responses to The Base Pollution argument are inadequate.

Wilson offers two responses. One is to reject Howell's claim that properties are individuated partly by their necessary features. Here she appeals again to her Malebranchean God scenario:

> Consider the scenario . . . in which a consistent Malebranchean God brings about mental features on the occasion of certain physical features in every world where the latter exist (that is, with metaphysical necessity). In such a scenario it need not be any part of 'what it is to be' the occasioning physical features that God takes them to be such occasions. (Wilson 2021, p. 147)

What should we make of that response? Howell's view about property individuation is controversial (Orilia and Paoletti 2022). So, it is fair of Wilson to question it. But her argument against it is directly challenged by his dilemma argument ("...did God have to make things this way or not?"), which I quoted five paragraphs back—an argument she does not address. Further, his view about property individuation might not be essential to The Base Pollution Argument. Perhaps his view helps him justify premise 1, which says that emergentism entails that the base properties either brutely necessitate mental properties or are infused with mentality in a way that renders them non-physical. But why couldn't he justify premise 1 on independent grounds, as follows?

> Sub-argument for premise 1
> Emergentism provides no resources for explaining why the base properties necessitate non-physical mental properties. That leaves us with two options: either the necessitation is brute, or the necessitated non-physical mentality is already present in the base properties.

That sub-argument does not rely on Howell's view about property individuation. Yet it seems to express the reasoning underlying premise 1 adequately.

Wilson's other response is to endorse one developed by Morris, who writes,

> The challenge for a supervenience physicalist is to account for the difference between the polluted base and a physical supervenience base without, in effect, rendering talk of supervenience superfluous in characterizing physicalism. This would fail to be the case if, as argued below, the only or best way to mark the requisite distinction appeals to the very resources at work in alternative formulations of physicalism or, likewise, alternative accounts of what it is to be a physicalist about some feature of reality. (Morris 2014, p. 357)

Morris goes on to do what he promises. He argues that accounting for the requisite distinction will require explaining the basis for the physicalist's supervenience thesis in terms of something more basic, such as a realization thesis. That in turn delivers a non-supervenience-based characterization of physicalism, thus "rendering talk of supervenience superfluous in characterizing physicalism." Wilson (2021, p. 147) writes, "I agree with Morris's assessment..."

But Wilson's use of Morris's argument as a counter to Howell's Base Pollution Argument is puzzling. Morris's argument does not seem to threaten Howell's. If sound, Morris's argument might show that physicalism cannot be adequately characterized solely in terms of supervenience. It does not follow that supervenience is not sufficient for physicalism, let alone that Howell's criticism of The Argument from Emergentism fails. To say that supervenience is sufficient for physicalism is to say that if supervenience holds, then physicalism is true. The latter, conditional claim concerns a consequence of supervenience for the truth value of physicalism, not for how physicalism can be characterized. The conditional claim might be true even if, as Morris writes, "talk of supervenience [is] superfluous in characterizing physicalism."

We should distinguish three claims:

(C1) The Argument from Emergentism fails to refute the claim that mental–physical supervenience is sufficient for physicalism.
(C2) Mental–physical supervenience is sufficient for physicalism.
(C3) Physicalism can be adequately characterized solely in terms of mental–physical supervenience.

The conclusion of Howell's Base Pollution Argument is C1 and C1 only. Morris's argument threatens C3 but not C1 (or C2).[8] Thus, neither of Wilson's responses to Howell's argument seems adequate.

C2 is not the conclusion of The Base Pollution Argument. But The Base Pollution Argument might help support an argument for C2 if we add a further premise: the premise that the only way to explain why the mental supervenes on the physical is to assume physicalism's truth. Howell does not assert that additional premise. But he does make a claim in its vicinity:

> It seems there is no other explanation [of mental–physical supervenience] than that it is part of the individuation conditions of the properties in the supervenience base to give rise to the supervening properties. (Howell 2013, p. 52)

Howell's claim suggests that the necessitation of the mental by the physical would have to be grounded solely in the base physical properties—rather than in, say, the power of a Malebranchean God or in fundamental emergence laws. And if such necessitation is grounded solely in the base physical properties, then physicalism might seem to follow. Or at least, it might then be hard to see how there could be a plausible counterexample

[8] Morris (2014, 2019) himself does not seem to disagree. My dispute here is only with Wilson (2021).

to C2. Nevertheless, in the next section, I will argue that there is such a counterexample.

4. The Argument from Neutral Monism

Suppose The Base Pollution Argument is sound and thus that emergentism is not a counterexample to C2, the claim that mental–physical supervenience is sufficient for physicalism. There is, I contend, another theory that can serve as such a counterexample: neutral monism. Thus, consider:

The Argument from Neutral Monism

1. Neutral monism, a non-physicalist theory, is consistent with PSV*.
2. If neutral monism is consistent with PSV*, then PSV* is not sufficient for physicalism.
3. Therefore, PSV* is not sufficient for physicalism.

That argument is valid. Is it sound? I think so. Premise 1 is plausible. According to neutral monism, the mental and the physical are both manifestations of a single, underlying, neutral reality. That theory is consistent with a variety of positions on how those manifestations interrelate, including the relationship expressed by PSV*—as premise 1 asserts. If neutral monism is true and the mental is necessitated by the physical, then that necessitation need not obtain ultimately in virtue of the nature of the physical. That is because, according to neutral monism, that physical nature is derivative: physical properties are grounded in neutral properties. The same is true of mental properties: they too are grounded in neutral properties, according to neutral monism. Nonetheless, a mental–physical supervenience thesis such as PSV* might obtain. That thesis would not be explained solely in physicalist terms. Instead, it would be explained partly by the fact that mental properties and physical properties share the same fundamental, neutral nature. Premise 2 is plausible too. Neutral monism is an alternative to (and inconsistent with) physicalism. Therefore, neutral monism's consistency with PSV* entails that PSV* is not sufficient for physicalism.

One might object to premise 1 as follows:

Objection to Premise 1

Neutral monism has essentially the same problem that emergentism has with respect to explaining how the mental could supervene on the physical.

> On neutral monism, the base properties are not infused with mentality. But they are infused with neutrality, which is just as bad. Pollution by neutral properties is still pollution. Neutral monism is therefore no more consistent with mental-physical supervenience than emergentism is. Premise 1 is false.

That objection might seem initially compelling. But it assumes a principle that is dialectically problematic: if a property P is physical, then P is not grounded in any non-physical property. Call that principle *No Non-Physical Grounding.* According to neutral monism, (i) there are physical properties and (ii) physical properties are grounded in neutral properties, which are non-physical.[9] The conjunction of (i) and (ii) directly conflicts with No Non-Physical Grounding. To assume the latter principle is tantamount to assuming that neutral monism is false. In the present context, where we are assessing whether PSV* is compatible with any non-physicalist theory, that move—assuming that neutral monism is false—should be off limits. It begs the question against proponents of such a compatibility claim, such as proponents of The Argument from Neutral Monism.

The objector might contend that No Non-Physical Grounding is independently plausible. But that seems doubtful. There is a weaker principle that is indeed independently plausible: if a property P is physical *and physicalism is true*, then P is not grounded in any non-physical property (at least not ultimately). Call that weaker principle *Weak No Non-Physical Grounding.* But Weak No Non-Physical Grounding does not apply unless we assume that physicalism is true—which would be question-begging in this context. So, Weak No Non-Physical Grounding cannot save the Objection to Premise 1. If No Non-Physical Grounding seems initially plausible, this impression may derive from mistaking it for the weaker version.

Unlike the neutral monist, the emergentist does not claim that physical properties are grounded in non-physical properties. On the contrary, emergentism (as I am using the term) is a version of dualism on which there are both physical properties, which are not grounded in anything other

[9] Although I formulate (i) and (ii) in terms of the existence of certain properties, they could instead be formulated in terms of the instantiation of those properties, as follows: (i) some physical properties are instantiated and (ii) those instantiations are grounded in instantiations of neutral properties, which are non-physical. Likewise, No Non-Physical Grounding could be formulated as follows: if a property P is physical, then no instantiation of P is grounded in an instantiation of any non-physical property. Here the differences between the existence-oriented and instantiation-oriented formulations do not matter much.

than the physical, and non-physical, emergent mental properties. That is why, if Howell is right, the emergentist cannot plausibly accept genuine mental–physical supervenience. If emergentism is true, then there would appear to be nothing about physical properties that would explain how they could metaphysically necessitate non-physical, emergent mental properties. Hence, the claim that, on emergentism, the base properties are infused with mentality: that infusion would help explain the metaphysical necessitation. The neutral monist faces no such difficulty. If her view is true, then there is something about physical properties that would explain how they could metaphysically necessitate mental properties. That something is (in part) that physical properties share the same fundamental nature with the mental properties that, if mental–physical supervenience holds, they necessitate.

It is not difficult to see how such an explanation could go. For example, it is consistent with neutral monism that mental properties are grounded in certain physical properties. Mental properties would not be *ultimately* so grounded. Neither would physical properties. According to neutral monism, both sorts of property are ultimately neutrally grounded. It is also consistent with neutral monism that mental properties are identical to certain physical properties. Either such a grounding thesis or such an identity thesis could explain mental–physical supervenience. Indeed, whatever the physicalist's preferred explanation of mental–physical supervenience is, the neutral monist can help herself to that explanation. She need only add that neutral properties underlie the physical properties invoked by that explanation.

Consider an analogy. A physicalist can accept the claim that *being a diamond* supervenes on *being a lattice of carbon atoms*. Moreover, she can accept that supervenience claim without saying either that the supervenience is brute or that the carbon atoms are infused with diamond-ness in a way that would render them not purely carbon. The supervenience claim could be explained by the claim that a diamond is grounded in a lattice of carbon atoms, and that grounding claim is consistent with the physicalist's claim that a lattice of carbon atoms is itself grounded in more basic physical phenomena. Likewise, a neutral monist can accept the claim that the mental supervenes on the physical. Moreover, she can accept that claim without saying either that the supervenience is brute or that the physical properties on which the mental supervene are infused with mentality in a way that would render them not purely physical. The claim that the mental supervenes on the physical could be explained by the claim that the mental is grounded in the physical, and that grounding claim is consistent with the neutral monist's claim that the physical is itself grounded in the neutral.

So, the objection to premise 1 of The Argument from Neutral Monism fails. I can see no viable objection to that premise or to premise 2. Thus, neutral monism would appear to be a genuine counterexample to the claim that mental–physical supervenience alone is sufficient for physicalism.

5. Conclusion

As Lewis suggests, it is not easy to define physicalism precisely. Many philosophers think that it cannot be defined solely in terms of a mental–physical supervenience thesis such as PSV*: supervenience may be necessary for physicalism, but it is not sufficient. I am sympathetic to that view. How to show it is another matter. Howell's Base Pollution Argument casts doubt on The Argument From Emergentism, according to which PSV* is not sufficient for physicalism because it is consistent with non-physicalist emergentism. I defended Howell's argument from Wilson's responses. But I explained how his argument can be sidestepped by replacing the claim that PSV* is consistent with emergentism with the claim that PSV* is consistent with neutral monism. Unlike emergentism, neutral monism provides resources for explaining how physical properties might metaphysically necessitate mental properties, without implying that physical properties are polluted in a way that renders them not genuinely physical. If that is correct, then the widely held view that supervenience is not sufficient for physicalism is vindicated. And that returns us to Lewis's challenge of finding a way to state physicalism precisely—a challenge I will address in Chapter 8.

8
Grounding Physicalism and Neocarn

In Chapter 7, I argued that the sort of mental–physical supervenience thesis associated with physicalism, such as PSV*, could be true even if physicalism is false. If so, then physicalism cannot be adequately characterized in terms of supervenience alone. In this chapter, I will do three things. First, I will consider whether physicalism can be adequately characterized by combining PSV* with the claim that the relevant base properties are primitive. Second, I will propose an alternative characterization, which appeals to (metaphysical) grounding instead of supervenience. The latter is by no means a new idea (Schaffer 2017).[1] On the contrary, as Shamik Dasgupta (2015, p. 557, fn. 1) notes, authors who suggest that philosophical doctrines such as physicalism should be understood in terms of grounding "take themselves to be reinvigorating a traditional conception of these issues that stems back at least to the ancient Greeks." My goal is only to connect a grounding-based approach with ideas that I develop in this book. Third, I will propose a new way to define what it means for something to be physical. I will begin with neocart, Howell's (2012, 2013) neo-Cartesian definition of a physical property. Neocart faces problems but, I will argue, they can be solved by modifying its formulation in two ways: allowing that the properties neocart describes might be underlain by more fundamental phenomena; and adding a neo-Carnapian necessary condition that all physical phenomena are structural.

1. Strengthened Supervenience

Before turning to grounding, I will briefly consider the possibility that I dismissed supervenience-based characterizations of physicalism too

[1] Nor is the idea uncontroversial. For criticisms, see, for example, Sider (2011), Daly (2012), Melnyk (2106), Wilson (2014), Koslicki (2015), and Fritz (2022). For defenses, see, for example, Audi (2012a, 2012b), Berker (2018), Cameron (2016), Ney (2016), and Schaffer (2016, 2017).

Monism Matters. Torin Alter, Oxford University Press. © Torin Alter 2026.
DOI: 10.1093/9780198931560.003.0009

hastily. In Chapter 7, I used The Argument from Neutral Monism to show that mental–physical supervenience is not sufficient for physicalism. But that argument can be circumvented by conjoining the relevant supervenience thesis with a claim concerning the base properties (that is, the physical* properties on which the mental are said to supervene):

Base Primitiveness. All properties in the supervenience base are primitive.

Call the conjunction of PSV* and Base Primitiveness *Strengthened Supervenience.* Unlike PSV*, Strengthened Supervenience is incompatible with neutral monism: if the physical properties in PSV*'s base are primitive, then they are not underlain by neutral properties. Thus, the Argument from Neutral Monism does not threaten Strengthened Supervenience. It seems plausible that Strengthened Supervenience is both necessary and sufficient for physicalism. Suppose it is. Could Strengthened Supervenience serve as an adequate characterization of physicalism?

Perhaps, at least for certain purposes. For example, Strengthened Supervenience could probably stand in for physicalism in the debate over whether PSV* and closely related theses are true—a debate in which The Conceivability Argument and related anti-physicalist arguments figure centrally.[2] Nevertheless, it would be preferable to formulate physicalism in a way that makes clear not only *that* the mental supervenes on the physical but also *why* that supervenience relation obtains.[3] That would make for a more illuminating definition. That goal is not achieved merely by conjoining Base Primitiveness with a supervenience thesis such as PSV*. But it might be achieved by appealing to grounding. Recall that grounding entails supervenience: if *x* grounds *y*, then *y* supervenes on *x*. Grounding might also help explain the supervenience theses it entails. So, for example, that a diamond is grounded in a lattice of carbon atoms might help explain why the former supervenes on the latter. Similarly, that the mental is grounded in the physical might help explain why PSV* obtains.[4] Let us therefore turn to an approach to defining physicalism that involves grounding.

[2] See Chapter 3, Section 2.

[3] Cf. Witmer (2020, p. 890); Stoljar (2022, sec. 2.1). Arguably, this is part of what the arguments of Horgan (1993) and others are meant to show.

[4] Whether the proposition that the mental is grounded in the physical *would* help in this regard is debatable (Wilson 2014). But the chances of it helping seem to me high enough to justify exploring the idea.

2. Grounding Physicalism

The core physicalist thesis could be stated in terms of grounding as follows, where to be *primitively physical* is to be *physical and ungrounded*:

> *Grounding Physicalism.* For all actual, concrete phenomena *x*, *x* is either primitively physical or ultimately grounded in only primitively physical phenomena.

In the next section, I will consider objections to taking Grounding Physicalism to be the core physicalist thesis. But first I will note that Grounding Physicalism has idealist, neutral monist, and dualist analogues. These can be stated in a parallel way, with appropriate substitutions and, in the case of Grounding Dualism, minor adjustments:

> *Grounding Idealism.* For all actual, concrete phenomena *x*, *x* is either primitively mental or ultimately grounded in only primitively mental phenomena.

> *Grounding Neutral Monism.* For all actual, concrete phenomena *x*, *x* is either primitively neutral or ultimately grounded in only primitively neutral phenomena.

> *Grounding Dualism.* All actual, concrete phenomena are either entirely mental, entirely physical, or partly mental and partly physical. For all actual, concrete mental phenomena *x*, *x* is either primitively mental or ultimately grounded in only primitively mental phenomena. For all actual, concrete physical phenomena *y*, *y* is either primitively physical or ultimately grounded in only primitively physical phenomena.[5]

3. Objections

In this section, I will consider three objections to taking Grounding Physicalism to be the core physicalist thesis. The first objection is that

[5] Grounding Dualism is not sufficient for Cartesian Dualism. But we could get closer to the latter by adding that all human minds are entirely mental, and all human bodies are entirely physical.

grounding is insufficiently specific for the task at hand: to say that the physical grounds the mental is unhelpful because it leaves open whether, for example, the mental reduces to the physical, is causally efficacious, or even exists.[6] But as Stoljar (2022, sec. 2.4) writes, "it may be a feature rather than a bug that grounding leaves these things open" (cf. Schaffer 2016). I concur. Physicalists should be able to argue among themselves about how to go beyond their core thesis and answer questions about reduction, mental causation, eliminativism/illusionism, etc.

A second objection arises from the opposite perspective. Here the concern is that, for the purpose of stating the core physicalist thesis, appealing to grounding is overly specific. For example, some physicalists might prefer to frame their view in terms of identity or realization rather than grounding. Thus, the objection runs, Grounding Physicalism is insufficiently ecumenical to qualify as the core physicalist thesis.

In response, I will argue that Grounding Physicalism (as I understand it) is consistent with those alternative formulations. Regarding identity, note that a mental–physical identity thesis alone need not entail physicalism. Consider the claim that mental property M is identical to physical property P. As I noted in Chapter 5, Section 6, one need not be a physicalist to accept that claim: an idealist could accept it too ("P is really just M"). So could a neutral monist ("P and M are identical, but both are really just N"). The claim becomes distinctively physicalist only when metaphysical priority is given to the physical side of the identity—that is, when the physical description is deemed as capturing the fundamental nature of the property more accurately than the mental description does ("M is really just P"). Indeed, even that is not enough. In principle, a neutral monist could also give metaphysical priority to the physical side of the identity over the mental side. To make the identity claim distinctively physicalist, the physical must be given metaphysical priority over all other candidates, including the neutral. Identity alone does not bestow the requisite priority. We need something that does, and grounding seems to fit the bill.

Other relations might also serve that purpose. For example, one might say that not only are M and P identical, but P explains M in a way that M does not

[6] Wilson (2014) develops an objection along these lines. However, she concludes only that grounding is useless "on its own" (Wilson 2014, p. 576). That conclusion is consistent with the position I take here. As I noted in Chapter 4, Section 5, I remain neutral on whether "grounding" names a distinctive, unified relation or rather a disjunction of more specific relations, such as constitution, realization, etc. My position is also consistent with Morris's (2019, p. 172) related argument that "when it comes to addressing the problems that plague nonreductive physicalism, primitive Grounding is thoroughly ineffective."

explain P. However, "explain" might indicate an epistemic relation, and here I assume that the core physicalist thesis is not epistemic but metaphysical.[7] "Explain" could instead be understood to express a metaphysical relation. But which metaphysical relation? Grounding is a plausible answer.

In any case, Grounding Physicalism is consistent with (but does not entail) the familiar mental–physical type-identity thesis on which, for example, pain is a brain state (Place 1956; Smart 1959; Lewis 1966; Armstrong 1968). That identity thesis does not settle how brain states relate to the most basic physical phenomena, given the plausible assumption that brain states are not among the latter. But Grounding Physicalism is also consistent with conceiving of that relationship too in terms of identity. For example, Grounding Physicalists could (but need not) hold that brain states are identical to configurations of certain basic physical phenomena.

What about the suggestion that, in characterizing the relationship between basic physical phenomena and other phenomena, some physicalists would refer to realization rather than to grounding? Here one issue is that realization is associated with functionalism, and physicalists need not accept functionalism. Realization can be disassociated from functionalism. But in that case, it is not clear how, or if, realization differs from grounding.[8] I have not said much about what grounding involves. I have said that it is an ontological dependence or existing-in-virtue-of relation, and that it would entail (and possibly account for) the claim that the mental supervenes on, but is not over and above, the physical.[9] That description might apply equally to a suitably ecumenical notion of realization.

A third objection is that Grounding Physicalism lacks certain advantages over dualism that physicalism is widely thought to enjoy (Pautz forthcoming). In particular, physicalism is thought to be more parsimonious than (interactionist) dualism, for example, with respect to laws of nature.[10] Unlike dualists, physicalists do not posit contingent psychophysical laws in addition to the fundamental physical truths. However, the objection runs, Grounding Physicalists posit grounding laws just as dualists do, and this undermines physicalism's parsimony claim. Unlike the dualist's psychophysical laws,

[7] See Chapter 1, Section 1.

[8] Cf. Stoljar (2022, sec. 2.3).

[9] See Chapter 4, Section 5.

[10] According to interactionist dualism, there is two-way mental–physical causation: from mental to physical, and from physical to mental (Alter and Howell 2012). There are other versions of dualism, such as epiphenomenalism, on which there is no mental-to-physical causation (Jackson 1982). Unless otherwise specified, by "dualism" I mean the interactionist variety.

grounding laws would hold in all possible worlds. Even so, says the objector, grounding laws would be additions to the fundamental physical truths, just as the dualist's psychophysical laws would be.

In response, I grant the objector's conditional premise: if Grounding Physicalists posit grounding laws that are over and above the fundamental physical truths, then Grounding Physicalism is no more parsimonious than dualism is, at least with respect to laws of nature. But I deny the antecedent. Admittedly, some take versions of physicalism that appeal to grounding to imply that such additional grounding laws exist (Schaffer 2017, Pautz forthcoming). But as I understand Grounding Physicalism, it has no such implication. There might well be grounding laws. Perhaps "A diamond is grounded in a lattice of carbon molecules" (or a more precise version of that statement) is an example. Yet if Grounding Physicalism is true, then any such grounding law would be entailed by the fundamental physical truths, not over and above them.[11] The physicalist's parsimony claim is not undermined.[12] More generally, I see no good reason to conclude that Grounding Physicalism lacks any advantage over dualism that physicalism is widely thought to enjoy.

4. Neocart

Grounding Physicalism addresses the domain problem: physicalism's domain includes *all and only actual, concrete phenomena.* Grounding Physicalism also addresses the relation problem: non-basic physical phenomena *identical to* or *ultimately grounded in* basic physical phenomena. What about the base problem? How should we understand what it means to be physical (or physical*)? The traditional Cartesian definition, that to be physical is to be spatially extended, is inadequate. In Chapter 6 (Sections 1 and 2), I raised problems for defining the physical negatively, as the not-fundamentally-mental, or deferentially, in terms of the posits of physics. I also used neocart, Howell's neo-Cartesian definition of physical properties, to illustrate what a viable non-deferential, positive definition of the physical

[11] That claim may be oversimple. Dasgupta (2015) argues that there are grounding facts that are consistent with physicalism even though they are neither fundamental physical facts nor grounded by fundamental physical facts. Facts in that third category are "not apt for being grounded." But the existence of such facts would not threaten the claim that Grounding Physicalism is more parsimonious than dualism.

[12] If Grounding Physicalism is true, would grounding laws be a priori deducible from the fundamental laws? Here I take no stand on that issue. See Chalmers and Jackson (2001) and Schaffer (2017).

might look like. In this section, I will raise problems for neocart. In the next section, I will propose an amended version.

Here might wonder why I start with neocart. After all, neocart is not the only positive, non-deferential definition of the physical that may be found in the contemporary literature. But I am aware of none that shows as much promise. Consider two examples. First, Ned Markosian (2000) proposes that physical objects are those that have spatial locations. But as Ney (2008, p. 8) argues, that definition threatens to undermine the distinction between physicalism and certain non-physicalist views, such as a dualist view on which non-physical substances or non-physical property instances have spatial locations—locations that might be determined by those of brains with which those substances and property instances are causally connected. A non-physical substance might share the location of an associated brain. And a non-physical property instance might share its location with a correlated neural property.

Second, Stoljar (2022, sec. 4.1) describes an "object-based conception" of the physical, according to which "A property is physical iff it is the sort of property had by paradigmatic physical objects and their constituents." But what are the paradigmatic physical objects? Rocks and trees? Quarks and leptons? As Montero (1999, p. 184) writes, "rocks and trees (as well as quarks and leptons) are identified as central cases only on the assumption that idealism is false." As she also argues, it is far from clear how to identify the relevant features that make the paradigmatic physical objects physical (Montero 1999, p. 184ff).[13]

Let us turn to neocart, according to which "A property is physical iff it can be fully characterized in terms of the conditions it places on the distribution of things in space over time" (Howell 2013, p. 24). This definition shares much with its inspiration, Descartes' definition of the physical (that is, matter/body) as three-dimensional spatial extension, and with Markosian's definition of the physical as having spatial location. All three definitions emphasize the role of space. But there are differences. Spatiality figures less directly into Howell's definition than into Descartes' and Markosian's. Unlike Descartes' definition, Howell's allows for physical phenomena that are not themselves extended in three dimensions. For Howell, non-extended phenomena can be physical, so long as their existence does not imply the existence of properties that cannot be exhaustively characterized in terms of their

[13] Cf. Howell (2013, pp. 19–20).

spatiotemporal implications. And unlike Markosian's definition, Howell's does not imply that having a spatial location is sufficient (or necessary) for being physical.

Note that, according to neocart, having spatiotemporal implications is not sufficient for being a physical property.[14] That is due to neocart's "it can be fully characterized" clause. If non-physical ghostly properties existed, they might have spatiotemporal implications. But such properties would not be fully characterizable by those implications. So, by neocart, they would not qualify as physical. Strictly speaking, neocart concerns only properties, as opposed to events, objects, etc. But it could be understood to apply indirectly to other phenomena. For example, a physical object might be defined roughly as one whose essential properties all conform to neocart.[15] On this broad understanding of neocart, physicalism entails that the fundamental nature of any actual, concrete phenomenon is exhausted by its spatiotemporal implications. So, for example, fundamentally there would be no more to being an electron than the role it plays in the "giant causal flux" that physics describes (Chalmers 1996, p. 153).

For a non-deferential, positive characterization of the physical, neocart might seem promising. But it faces objections. For one thing, it might imply that all physical* properties are dispositional. At least, that is a natural way of understanding what it means for a property to be fully characterizable "in terms of the conditions it places on the distribution of things in space over time." On that understanding, such conditions concern dispositions that properties bestow on their bearers, that is, how things are disposed to be spatiotemporally distributed under such-and-such circumstances. However, the objection runs, physicalism should allow that physical* properties might include non-dispositional properties.

Neocart is compatible with the existence of physical properties that are non-dispositional, provided that those non-dispositional properties are not fundamental. For example, consider the chemical structure that serves as the categorical basis of a ceramic vase's fragility. That chemical structure could be described as non-dispositional. But that is consistent with neocart, because the chemical structure is not a *basic* physical property, that is, it is not physical*. Some would argue that the chemical structure consists in

[14] *Contra* Montero (2024, p. 237).

[15] This definition is rough. For example, a physical object might have the property of *being necessarily distinct from the number 37*, and the latter property does not appear to concern spacetime. In response, one might argue that no such property is essential to a physical object (Fine 1994). But the matter is complex.

physical* properties that are dispositional (Blackburn 1990). Perhaps it does. But Neocart seems to entail that *all* fundamental physical properties are dispositional, and that might be overly restrictive.[16] Some versions of physicalism posit non-dispositional, categorical properties that underlie fundamental physical dispositions (e.g., Lewis 2001; Brown 2017b). Arguably, such versions should not be ruled out as non-physicalist by definition.[17]

An obvious solution would be to add a clause to neocart stating that physical properties might include categorical properties that underlie relevant dispositional properties (that is, those whose natures are exhausted by their spatiotemporal implications). But that addition will not quite do, at least not by itself. Not all candidates for such underlying categorical properties are physicalism friendly. For example, primitively mental categorical properties would not be.

Howell recognizes this problem. In response, he distinguishes the sorts of categorical properties that physicalists can countenance from those they cannot. He begins by introducing the notion of a *Trans-World Disposition Set (TDS)*:

> Each property confers a set of dispositions within a world. The TDS of a property is the set of dispositions the property gives rise to in each world. So, for example, charge gives rise to a certain group of dispositions D[1] in world 1, but a different set of dispositions D2 in world 2, etc. The TDS for charge can be characterized as a set of pairs of worlds and dispositions {<w1, D1>, <w2, D2>...<wn, Dn>}. Even if the powers of a property differ from world to world, its TDS does not—it is a necessary feature of the property. (Howell 2013, p. 29)

Howell then proceeds to distinguish "thick" and "thin" properties. He writes, "thin properties obey the following individuation principle: . . . If the TDS of P1 and P2 are the same, then P1 = P2" (Howell 2013, p. 29; cf. Shoemaker 1980). By contrast, thick properties do not obey that individuation principle. Physical properties include only thin properties. Howell also suggests that the nature of a thin physical property can be fully characterized

[16] Could all basic properties be dispositional? Perhaps. See McKitrick (2003), Ladyman and Ross (2007).

[17] According to these versions, the relevant categorical properties are ontologically distinct from the dispositions they underlie. Neocart has no trouble accommodating an alternative version, according to which that ontological distinctness claim is false (Heil 2003).

in terms of its TDS.[18] If so, then not only are thin properties *individuated* by their TDS's: their TDS's fully capture their natures.[19] This leads Howell to propose a revised version of neocart:

> *Neocart-con:* A property P is physical, iff (a) in the actual world P confers only spatio-temporal powers upon its bearer, and (b) P is a thin property. (Howell 2013, p. 30)[20]

In effect, neocart-con counts properties as physical if and only if their natures can be fully characterized in terms of their spatiotemporal dispositions *across possible worlds*. This allows for the existence of physical (or physical*) properties that are categorical, as long as they are thin. And because primitively mental categorical properties would be thick, they do not qualify as physical. Thus, moving from neocart to neocart-con helps.

But that move leaves part of the problem unsolved. Lewis (2001) advocates a version of physicalism on which there are quiddities: categorical properties that underlie the dispositional properties posited by ideal physics. Further, according to Lewis, distinct quiddities differ from each other only with respect to their numerical identity.[21] Distinct quiddities underlie different dispositions, but only contingently. For example, if in the actual world quiddity Q1 underlies mass and quiddity Q2 underlies charge, then there is another possible world in which Q1 underlies charge and Q2 underlies mass. Distinct Lewisian quiddities do not differ from each other with respect to

[18] Howell (2013, p. 30) writes, "A physicalist should allow only thin properties in the base. To embrace thick properties, one must believe that there is some feature of a property that is over and above that which is necessitated by the powers the property contributes. For my part, the only intrinsic feature I can think of that is suited for this job is an intrinsic feel or quale, but whatever it is it would of necessity be beyond the pale of any possible science and could have no explanatory value. Any physicalist worth her salt should steer clear of such things."

[19] That the nature of a physical property P's is fully captured by its TDS does not entail that its nature reduces to its TDS. In particular, one might accept the former claim and also identify basic physical properties with intrinsic aptnesses. Such intrinsic aptnesses would explain why those properties have the TDS's that they have. Shoemaker (1980, p. 115) suggests a position along those lines, and it seems consistent with Howell's position.

[20] Howell (2013, p. 30) calls this version "neocart-con" because it is designed "for the theorist who believes properties have their powers only contingently" (hence "con," for "contingent"). For present purposes, however, the crucial issue is not whether properties have their powers contingently or necessarily but rather how to ensure that any categorical properties that qualify as physical are physicalism friendly.

[21] At least, this is how Lewisian quiddities are often understood. See Lewis (2001, sec. 4), Stoljar (2014, p. 24), Chalmers (2012, p. 349). Lewisian quiddities should not be confused with Russellian quiddities. It is not the case that distinct Russellian quiddities differ from each other only with respect to their numerical identity. See Chapter 1, Section 3.

their TDS's. In Howell's terminology, they are thick.[22] Therefore, neocart-con entails that they are not physical. That result is undesirable. Lewis regards quiddities as physical, and that seems reasonable. At least, it seems that such quiddities could be physical. After all, Lewis posits them in order to account for the phenomena described by fundamental physics, and they bear no special relation to mental phenomena.

I will return to this problem shortly. First, let me describe another objection to neocart. This objection centers on the idea that spacetime might turn out to be derivative. As Howell puts it,

> Apparently some physicists claim it is a live hypothesis that classical space-time is emergent. . . While this might not threaten the truth of our space-time talk, it does threaten the claim that physical properties can be exhaustively characterized by their spatio-temporal implications. After all, if space and time emerge from some lower domain, presumably that lower domain cannot itself be fully characterized in spatio-temporal terms, and yet surely the properties there deserve to be called physical if they are posited by our best physics. So, my definition is inadequate. (Howell 2013, p. 34)

In response, Howell considers different versions of the view that classical space-time is emergent and argues that some of them are inconsistent with physicalism, including one on which the emergence is brute. He also writes,

> . . . the way many physicists seem to put the issue is in terms of the emergence of "classical" space-time. This leaves open the possibility that classical space-time emerges from another state space that is non-classical. For example, there is the suggestion that the Riemannian structure of classical space-time could be seen as emerging from a more fundamental, infinite dimensional Hilbert space. . . If this is the case, the spatio-temporal definition is only threatened if it is wedded to characterizing things in terms of classical space-time. But there is no need to limit it in this way. The essence of the definition would remain intact, for example, if it turned out

[22] Lewisian quiddities are thick in Howell's sense, because they are not individuated by their TDS's. But Lewisian quiddities are not thick in Chalmers's (2012, p. 350) sense, according to which thick quiddities "have a substantial nature of some sort and are not merely numerically distinct from each other." Russellian quiddities are thick in Chalmers's sense. Are they thick in Howell's sense? This is not clear. Russellian monists might or might not tie specific quiddities to specific dispositions (Alter and Coleman 2021).

> that physical properties were those that are exhaustively defined by their implications for the distribution of things and properties over a Hilbert space. The definition can be viewed as flexible, with no loss to my purposes, substituting the more fundamental space for the classical space-time. (Howell 2013, p. 34)

Howell's response seems reasonable. But it is designed to address one specific possibility: "the Riemannian structure of classical space-time could be seen as emerging from a more fundamental, infinite dimensional Hilbert space." Yet the problem seems more general. The challenge is to accommodate the possibility that spacetime is constituted by more basic phenomena of some or other physicalism-friendly kind—a kind that might or might not have something to do with infinite-dimensional Hilbert space.[23] In responding to that problem, we should be as non-committal as possible regarding the nature of those more basic phenomena.

There is also a related problem. We need to ensure that neocart properties themselves are not primitively mental or otherwise physicalism unfriendly. After all, an idealist could accept that all actual, concrete phenomena conform to neocart but add that the fundamental nature of spacetime is mental.

So, neocart faces at least three problems: how to count physicalism-friendly categorical properties (such as Lewisian quiddities) as physical, without counting physicalism-unfriendly categorical properties as physical; how to allow for the possibility that spacetime is derivative but physicalism friendly, without committing specifically to the Hilbert-space version of that possibility; and how to ensure that neocart phenomena are not identified with phenomena that are not physicalism friendly, as would be the case if, as an idealist might argue, spacetime itself is fundamentally mental.[24]

[23] Even that more general formulation is too narrow. It implies that spacetime exists, and we should allow for the possibility that spacetime is an illusion. The amended version of neocart that I will propose in Section 5 can do that, if in that version references to space and time are qualified with "or appearances thereof."

[24] Howell (2013, pp. 31–37) addresses other objections to neocart, in addition to those I have mentioned. Here is one more that he does not raise: "Neocart refers to "the distribution of things in space over time." But space (or spacetime) itself is not a thing in space. Isn't that physical? How can neocart account for this?" In response, Howell might argue that, although space itself is not a thing in space, space can nonetheless be fully characterized in terms of the conditions it places on the distribution of things in space over time. Alternatively, he could amend neocart by adding a disjunct: "or is the property of being space (or spacetime)." Doing so would not be ad hoc. After all, he states neocart in terms of notions of space and time that he assumes are physicalism friendly. Assuming that space (or spacetime) itself qualifies as physical comports with that neo-Cartesian approach.

5. From neocart to neocarn

A partial solution to the three problems facing neocart suggests itself: we could define the physical in such a way as to allow for two epistemic possibilities. One possibility is that the physical phenomena are those that neocart-con describes. Another is that there are phenomena that underlie those that neocart-con describes. The only remaining challenge is to find a way of ensuring that all such phenomena are physicalism friendly.

To address that challenge, I propose beginning with the following claim: all physical phenomena are structural, in a sense associated with Carnap (1928/1967) and more recently articulated by Chalmers (1996, 2010, 2012, 2013, 2020a).[25] On this view, the nature of any physical phenomenon can be fully characterized in terms of structural information, where structural information is information that can be fully expressed in mathematical, logical, nomic, and perhaps spatiotemporal terms.[26] That is plausibly true of all physical phenomena recognized by standard versions of physicalism.[27]

Howell's thin categorical properties are structural. Their natures can be fully characterized by their TDS's, which include only structural information. Lewisian (2001) quiddities too are plausibly structural.[28] To see this,

[25] Unless otherwise specified, by "structural" I mean structural in Chalmers's neo-Carnapian sense.

[26] Recall how Chalmers (2013, p. 256) characterizes structural properties: "a structural property is one that can be fully characterized using structural concepts alone, which I take to include logical, mathematical, and nomic concepts, perhaps along with spatiotemporal concepts . . . " Carnap (1928/1967, §6, p. 16) writes, "it will be demonstrated that it is in principle possible to characterize all objects through merely structural properties (that is, certain formal-logical properties of relation extensions or complexes of relation extensions) and thus to transform all scientific statements into purely structural statements." For discussion of the proposition that all physical phenomena are structural, see Stoljar (2015, 2020a), Alter (2016, 2023), Chalmers (2020a), and Alter and Pereboom (2023b).

[27] Nomic concepts such as *cause* and *law* should be understood to refer to causation and lawhood independently of roles those concepts play in physical theory. Otherwise, such concepts might be definable in terms of mathematical and logical concepts, in which case we might run into a version of a problem Max Newman (1928) raises for Russell's (1927) structuralist view about physics. Roughly, Newman argues that if every basic concept in physical theory were defined in terms of mathematical and logical concepts, then physical theory could be satisfied by virtually any set of the appropriate cardinality and would therefore be nearly vacuous. But as Russell (1951, p. 271) recognizes, the problem Newman identifies can be avoided by including in physical theory certain primitives that are not defined in terms of their roles in that theory. Such primitives could include nomic concepts (Chalmers 2020a).

[28] There are other ways to understand "structure" according to which Lewisian quiddities are non-structural. For example, structural properties could be understood as either extrinsic (relational) properties or what Pereboom (2019) calls relatively intrinsic properties, where "P is a *relatively intrinsic* property of X just in case P is an intrinsic property of X and P is grounded in extrinsic properties of parts of X" (Pereboom 2019, p. 184; italics in original). Arguably, Lewisian quiddities are not extrinsic or relatively intrinsic.

note two things. First, the *underlying* relation they would bear to basic physical dispositions can be fully characterized in terms of structural information. At least, that seems plausible given that nomic terms are allowed. Second, because mathematical and logical terms are also allowed, it is also plausible that the differences between distinct quiddities, which are merely numerical, can be expressed structurally. Likewise for infinite-dimensional Hilbert space: plausibly, it too is structural. By contrast, arguably anything that is primitively mental is not structural. That is, primitively mental phenomena are not structural in the sense I have described: their natures cannot be fully characterized in terms of structural information. This does not exclude the possibility that primitively mental phenomena have structural features. Plausibly, they do. But such features do not exhaust their natures.[29]

Although being structural is plausibly necessary for being physical, being structural is not sufficient for being physical. For example, being a prime number is a structural property but, arguably, it is not a physical property. Consider also Lewisian quiddities. If they are physical, this is not merely because they are structural. It is also because of how they are said to relate to the rest of the physical world, namely, by underlying physical dispositions.

We are now positioned to amend neocart. I will call the amended version *neocarn* ("carn" for Carnap):

> *Neocarn.* x is *physical* $=_{\text{df}}$ (i) x is structural and either (ii) x can be fully characterized in terms of the conditions x places on the distribution of things in space over time, across possible worlds (if phenomena that can be so characterized are not underlain by more basic phenomena) or (iii) x underlies phenomena that can be fully characterized in such terms.[30]

Neocarn is essentially a qualified version of neocart-con. Clause (ii) corresponds to neocart-con plus the conditional clause, "if the phenomena that can be so characterized are not underlain by more basic phenomena." Clause (iii) allows for phenomena underlying spacetime. Clause (i) addresses

[29] What about haecceities? A haecceity is the "primitive thisness" of an individual object (Kaplan 1975, pp. 722–23; Adams 1979). If haecceities exist, are they structural in the sense I have described? Perhaps. If they are construed as being analogous to Lewisian quiddities—if there is nothing more to their natures than their individuating function—then plausibly they are structural in that sense. But they might instead be construed as having a substantive, non-structural nature (cf. Lewis 1986, pp. 239–40). In that case, they may well not be structural.

[30] On option (iii), presumably physical phenomena could be fully characterized using only mathematical, logical, and nomic terms: spatiotemporal terms would not be needed. See Alter (2016) and Chalmers (2020a).

the concern about physicalism-unfriendly phenomena, such as primitively mental phenomena, counting as physical because they satisfy the conditions stated in clauses (ii) or (iii). If primitively mental phenomena are not structural—if the nature of such phenomena cannot be fully characterized in terms of structural information—then they do not satisfy clause (i).

Although neocarn describes two possibilities, (ii) and (iii), this need not make the category of the physical disunified. It seems plausible that either the phenomena clause (ii) describes are underlain by more basic phenomena or they are not. If they are, then clause (iii) applies. If they are not, then clause (ii) applies. Arguably, either way all neocarn phenomena share a substantive, unified, fundamental physical nature. But suppose that both (ii) and (iii) apply: that some neocart properties are underlain by more basic properties, while other neocart properties are not. In that case, one could argue that both sorts of properties, though distinct, share a deeper unity: both are structural, and both bear one or another fundamental relation to spacetime.[31]

Consider:

> *Grounding Physicalism, Neocarn Version.* For all actual, concrete phenomena *x*, *x* is either primitively physical or ultimately grounded only in primitively physical phenomena, where the physical is defined by neocarn.

I propose Grounding Physicalism, Neocarn Version as a candidate for the core thesis to which all standard versions of physicalism are committed.

The "standard" qualification is needed. At least some non-standard versions of physicalism do not entail Grounding Physicalism, Neocarn Version. For example, consider Russellian physicalism, the physicalist version of Russellian monism. Russellian monism posits non-structural quiddities. The latter are unlike Lewisian quiddities in that they "have a substantial nature of some sort and are not merely numerically distinct from each other" (Chalmers 2012, p. 350). According to Russellian physicalism, those quiddities are (in some sense) physical. But they are not physical in the neocarn sense: they are not structural.[32] Another example is Galen

[31] Is neocarn an adequate definition of the physical, for the purposes of defining physicalism and its rivals? It is difficult to have much confidence in that claim, given the poor track record of other such attempts. Even so, neocarn seems worth considering, at least as an improved version of neocart.

[32] Similar reasoning applies to haecceities (see fn. 29). If they are construed as analogous to *Lewisian* quiddities, then their existence is compatible with standard physicalism. If they are instead construed as analogous to *Russellian* quiddities, then their existence is not compatible with standard physicalism.

Strawson's (2008) "real materialism," according to which physical reality is irreducibly experiential. Irreducibly experiential phenomena are not structural either.

Does it follow that Russellian physicalism and Strawsonian real materialism are not genuine versions of physicalism? This issue seems merely verbal.[33] That is, it seems arbitrary whether we count Russellian physicalism and Strawsonian real materialism as genuine versions of physicalism. In any case, I claim only that Grounding Physicalism, Neocarn Version might capture the core thesis of standard physicalism. Even if Russellian physicalism and Strawsonian real materialism are *genuine* versions of physicalism, they are not *standard* versions.[34]

6. Conclusion

In Chapter 7, I used The Argument from Neutral Monism to show that mental–physical supervenience claims such as PSV* are not sufficient for physicalism. I began the present chapter by considering a view that The Argument from Neutral Monism does not threaten: Strengthened Supervenience, which conjoins PSV* and the claim that the base properties in PSV* are primitive. Strengthened supervenience might be truth-functionally equivalent to the core physicalist thesis. Nevertheless, I argued, Strengthened Supervenience might fall short of an adequate characterization of that thesis. That is because it is not clear that Strengthened Supervenience would explain why the mental supervenes on the physical*.

That led me to propose characterizing the core physicalist thesis as Grounding Physicalism, on which everything in the domain is or is ultimately grounded in primitively physical phenomena. I characterized Grounding Idealism, Grounding Neutral Monism, and Grounding Dualism analogously. Then I defended taking Grounding Physicalism to express the core physicalist thesis from three objections. Finally, I turned

[33] Recall Chalmers's test, discussed in Chapter 6, Section 3: "To adjudicate whether this dispute is verbal, one can bar 'physicalism', introduce 'physicalism$_1$' and 'physicalism$_2$', and see whether there is a residual disagreement" (Chalmers 2011, pp. 17–18). As applied to this case, I can see no such residual disagreement.

[34] One indication of this is that neither Russellian physicalism nor Strawsonian real materialism are threatened by anti-physicalist arguments such as The Knowledge Argument (Chalmers 1996, 2010; Alter 2023).

to the problem of how to characterize the physical. I proposed an amended version of neocart that I called neocarn. According to neocarn, physical phenomena are structural phenomena that are or underlie phenomena that can be fully characterized in terms of their transworld spatiotemporal implications.

9
Concluding Thoughts

In this last chapter, I will do two things. First, I will succinctly summarize the main arguments for and against the monism-matters thesis, which I presented in Chapters 2–6. Second, I will argue that considerations about monism might have implications for a debate in meta-ethics between moral realists and moral anti-realists—a debate that, in certain respects, parallels the debate in the philosophy of mind between dualists and physicalists.

1. Recap

In Chapter 1, I stated the core thesis of type monism as follows: (MT) All actual, concrete phenomena are such that there is exactly one unified, substantive, fundamental nature that they share. I also stated the monism-matters thesis as follows: considerations about monism figure importantly in the contemporary mind-body debate. In Chapter 2, I defended the latter thesis from three arguments. The first two can be stated roughly as follows:

- Monism does not matter because its truth or falsity depends on type-individualism, which is interest relative and therefore arbitrary.
- The only non-arbitrary ways of individuating types entail that the monism-matters thesis is false.

In response, I noted that MT and the monism-matters thesis concern *fundamental* types, and I argued that how fundamental types are individuated is not arbitrary in a way that threatens the monism-matters thesis.

The third argument against the monism-matters thesis can be stated roughly as follows:

- Monism does not matter because, when it comes to ontology, philosophers should defer to physics, which says nothing about monism.

Monism Matters. Torin Alter, Oxford University Press.
DOI: 10.1093/9780198931560.003.0010

I distinguished four versions of that last argument, each of which emphasizes one of the following claims:

- Physics is neutral on whether monism is true or false.
- No a priori constraints should be placed on what counts as physical.
- Ideal physics might posit fundamentally disunified phenomena.
- Monism is inextricably tied to an anachronistic conception of the physical.

In response, I conceded that there is something to each of those claims. For example, the claim that philosophers should not place a priori constraints on what counts as physical is motivated by an eminently reasonable concern: we should be reluctant to constrain the physical in a way that future empirical discoveries might undermine. After all, that is the fate that befell historically influential definitions of the physical, such as Descartes'. However, I argued, that reasonable concern does not justify a blanket exclusion of all a priori constraints. I argued that such a blanket exclusion constitutes an implausible overcorrection. More generally, I argued, when any of the four claims listed above is developed into an argument against the monism-matters thesis, the result is not convincing.

In Chapters 3 through 6, I gave six arguments for the monism-matters thesis:

- Detaching monism from physicalism, idealism, or neutral monism would undermine part of the motivation for those theories (Chapter 3).
- Physicalism, idealism, and neutral monism entail certain supervenience theses partly because those theories are versions of monism (Chapters 3 and 4).
- Physicalism, idealism, and neutral monism entail certain repudiation theses partly because those theories are versions of monism (Chapter 5).
- Considerations about monism help determine whether, for the purposes of the mind-body debate, *via negativa* physicalism is tenable (Chapter 6).
- Considerations about monism help determine whether, for the purposes of the mind-body debate, deferential definitions of the physical are tenable (Chapter 6).
- Considerations about monism help determine whether, for the purposes of the mind-body debate, the issue of whether physicalism is

compatible with the existence of fundamental mentality is merely verbal (Chapter 6).

Any one of those six arguments would suffice to establish the monism-matters thesis. Taken together, they make the case for it all the more compelling.

2. Monism and moral realism

The contemporary mind-body debate concerns the relationship between the mental and the physical. One central issue in the debate is whether physicalism can accommodate certain mental features, such as consciousness. Another challenge to physicalism concerns moral properties. Plausibly, at least some moral properties are instantiated. There are morally good (and bad) agents, morally permissible (and impermissible) actions, and so on. According to a view that William J. FitzPatrick (2022) calls "ardent moral realism," moral properties are irreducibly normative. They do not consist entirely in non-normative properties, that is, in properties that "could at least in principle be fully characterized in nonevaluative/nonnormative terms" (FitzPatrick 2022, p. 35). Is ardent moral realism compatible with physicalism? I will argue that monism is relevant to answering that question. Specifically, the idea that physicalism is a version of monism complicates attempts to reconcile moral realism with physicalism.

Sometimes the term "moral realism" is used for a view that is weaker than ardent moral realism. For example, sometimes the term refers to the view that there are moral truths, or to the view that there are moral truths that are not relative to either individual opinions or social conventions. Those weaker views are consistent with the claim that, in some important sense, moral truths reduce to non-normative truths.[1] Here I have in mind the stronger view, which is not consistent with such reductionist claims. But I will henceforth omit the "ardent" qualification and assume it is understood.

The question of whether moral realism and physicalism are compatible is sometimes taken to be connected to a related issue: whether moral realism conflicts with philosophical naturalism. Following William J. FitzPatrick's (2022) pellucid discussion, here we can think of naturalism as the view that, in the concrete world, the (instantiated) properties and facts include only

[1] For an example of this weaker version, see Foot (1972).

natural ones. As he explains, it is fairly common to understand what is meant by *natural* properties and facts as follows: "those that are in principle empirically investigable by the natural and social sciences or at least constructible from and exhaustively constituted by properties and facts that are" (FitzPatrick 2022, p. 34). On that characterization of naturalness, naturalism seems to conflict with the existence of irreducibly normative properties. As FitzPatrick explains,

> There is, on that [naturalist] picture, *no irreducibly evaluative or normative reality* on the scene: just ordinary empirical properties, perhaps grouped in complex ways, for which we have certain special terms and concepts that we give special practical and perhaps explanatory roles. That does not get us anything like the . . . moral realist's . . . irreducibly normative properties and facts in the world . . . (FitzPatrick 2022, p. 35; italics in original)

On that way of understanding naturalness, moral realism comes out as a non-naturalist theory (FitzPatrick 2008, 2022; Enoch 2011). This is sometimes taken to count against moral realism. Non-naturalistic moral properties are sometimes described as mysterious, even "spooky" (Gibbard 2003, p. 16; Jackson 1998, p. 127). They are said to be "divorced from our ethical concepts" and to "belong . . . to some other, mysterious 'non-natural' realm" (FitzPatrick 2022, p. 36). Reasonably enough, some doubt that such properties exist (Gibbard 2003; Jackson 1998).

But the latter description of the properties moral realists posit is inaccurate and misleading. As FitzPatrick explains,

> We [moral realists] are not trotting out some new, obscure property . . . divorced from our ethical concepts, to do mysterious work . . . . All we are doing is making a familiar normative claim about a set of ethical standards—that it is the appropriate one for ethical evaluation and for guiding human deliberation and action—and then maintaining that this claim states an irreducibly normative truth about that world . . . (FitzPatrick 2022, p. 36)

FitzPatrick suggests that it might be less misleading to expand the notion of naturalness so as to not necessarily exclude irreducibly normative phenomena. If the notion is so expanded, then moral realists can be naturalists. According to naturalistic moral realism, "There is *one reality*, the natural world, that happens to be ontologically rich enough to include inherently evaluative and normative aspects of things as well as scientifically transparent ones" (FitzPatrick 2022, p. 36; italics in original).

FitzPatrick's suggestion is reasonable. But moral realism—even the naturalistic variety—seems hard to reconcile with physicalism, if physicalism is a version of monism. Consider the fundamental nature of the natural properties moral realists posit. If monist physicalism is true, then such properties must share the same substantive, unified physical fundamental nature with all other actual, concrete phenomena. It is not clear how that could be. As I have argued, the claim that there is a single such nature entails that all actual, concrete phenomena are grounded in the most fundamental physical phenomena, that is, in physical* phenomena. So, if physicalism is true, then irreducibly normative phenomena are either (i) grounded in physical* phenomena or (ii) among the physical* phenomena. But claim (i) seems to conflict with the moral realist's denial that moral properties consist entirely in non-normative properties. Claim (ii) faces a different problem. If physicalism is true, then the fundamental physical nature that all concrete phenomena share is substantive and unified. It is hard to see how both moral properties, such as moral badness, and physical* properties such as mass and charge could share a unified, substantive nature. For example, moral badness does not appear to conform to neocarn. That moral property seems neither structural, nor fully characterizable in terms of its spatiotemporal implications, nor to consist in properties underlying properties that are fully characterizable in terms of their spatiotemporal implications.

This problem might not be insurmountable. Some argue that familiar doubts about the physical explicability of consciousness will dissipate as cognitive science advances (Weisberg 2025). One might take a similar tack here and argue that doubts about the physical explicability of moral features will dissipate as knowledge of nature and morality increases. Further, because monism, as I have explicated it, concerns concrete phenomena only, a second strategy would be to deny that moral phenomena are concrete. Third, perhaps moral realists with physicalist inclinations could settle for the view that physicalism is the correct theory with respect to the mental–physical relationship but not with respect to the moral–physical relationship.

Whether those or other strategies could work remains to be seen. For now, moral realism and physicalism would appear to be at odds with each other. This is not because of anything to do with naturalism. Instead, the apparent conflict derives partly from physicalism's being a version of monism. The same issue arises with respect to other versions of monism. For example, moral realism would also appear to conflict with idealism. Thus, there might be cause for expanding the monism-matters thesis. Not only does monism matter for the mind-body debate. It might matter for other philosophical debates, including the debate over moral realism.

References

Adams, R. M. 2021. *What Is, & What Is in Itself: A Systematic Ontology*. Oxford: Oxford University Press.

Adams, R. M. 1979. Primitive thisness and primitive identity. *Journal of Philosophy* 76 (1): 5–26.

Alter, T. 2024. Physicalism and fundamental mentality. *Synthese* 204 (6), URL = <https://doi.org/10.1007/s11229-024-04697-7>.

Alter, T. 2023. *The Matter of Consciousness: From the Knowledge Argument to Russellian Monism*. Oxford: Oxford University Press.

Alter, T. 2022. Physicalism without fundamentality. *Erkenntnis* 87: 1975–86.

Alter, T. 2021. A defense of the supervenience requirement on physicalism. *Thought: A Journal of Philosophy* 10 (4): 264–74.

Alter, T. 2016. The structure and dynamics argument against materialism. *Noûs* 50 (4), December: 794–815. 10.1111/nous.12134.

Alter, T., and Coleman, S. 2021. Russellian monism and mental causation. *Noûs* 55 (2), June: 409–25.

Alter, T., Coleman, S., and Howell, R. J. 2022. Physicalism, infinite decomposition, and constitution. *Erkenntnis* 89 (4): 1735–1744.

Alter, T., and Howell, R. J. 2022. Physicalism, supervenience, and monism. *Synthese* 200 (6): 1–19.

Alter, T., and Howell, R. J. (eds.) 2012. *Consciousness and the Mind-Body Problem: A Reader*. New York: Oxford University Press.

Alter, T., and Nagasawa, Y. 2012. What is Russellian monism? *Journal of Consciousness Studies* 19: 67–95.

Alter, T. and Pereboom, D. 2023a. Russellian monism. *The Stanford Encyclopedia of Philosophy* (Fall 2023 Edition), E. N. Zalta and U. Nodelman (eds.), URL = <https://plato.stanford.edu/archives/fall2023/entries/russellian-monism/>.

Alter, T. and Pereboom, D. 2023b. Russellian monism and structuralism about physics. *Erkenntnis* 88: 1409–28.

Aristotle. ca. 350 B. C. E./1953. *Metaphysics*. Trans. W. D. Ross. Oxford: Oxford University Press.

Aristotle. ca. 350 B. C. E./1984. *De Anima*. In J. Barnes (ed.) *The Complete Works of Aristotle*, Volumes I and II. Princeton: Princeton University Press.

Armstrong, D. 1968. *A Materialist Theory of Mind*. London: Routledge and Kegan Paul.

Audi, P. 2012a. Grounding: Toward a theory of the in-virtue-of relation. *The Journal of Philosophy* 109: 685–711.

Audi, P. 2012b. A clarification and defense of the notion of grounding. In F. Correia and B. Schneider (eds.) *Metaphysical Grounding*. Cambridge: Cambridge University Press: 101–221.

Avenarius, R. 1888/1890. *Kritik der Reinen Erfahrung*, Leipzig: Fues (R. Reisland).

Ball, D. 2009. There are no phenomenal concepts. *Mind* 118: 935–62.

Balog, K. 2012. A defense of the phenomenal concept strategy. *Philosophy and Phenomenological Research* 84: 1–23.

Baltimore, J. A. 2013. Careful, physicalists: Mind-body supervenience can be too super-duper. *Theoria*, 79 (1): 8–21.

Berker, S. 2018. The unity of grounding. *Mind* 127 (507): 729–77.

Berkeley, G. 1710. *A Treatise concerning the principles of human knowledge*. In A. Luce and T. Jessop (eds.) *The Works of George Berkeley, Bishop of Cloyne*. London: Thomas Nelson and Sons. vols 9, 1948–57.

Berryman, S. 2022. Ancient atomism. *The Stanford Encyclopedia of Philosophy* (Winter 2022 Edition), Edward N. Zalta and Uri Nodelman (eds.), URL = <https://plato.stanford.edu/archives/win2022/entries/atomism-ancient/>.

Bird, A. 2007. *Nature's Metaphysics: Laws and Properties*. Oxford: Oxford University Press.

Blackburn, S. 1990. Filling in space. *Analysis* 50: 62–65.

Bliss, R. and Trogdon, K. 2021. Metaphysical grounding. In *The Stanford Encyclopedia of Philosophy* (Winter 2021 Edition), Edward N. Zalta (ed.), URL = <https://plato.stanford.edu/archives/win2021/entries/grounding/>.

Block, N. 2006. Max Black's objection to mind-body identity. In R. Zimmerman (ed.) *Oxford Studies in Metaphysics*, Volume 2. New York: Oxford University Press: 3–78.

Bowyer, A. J. n. d. The via negativa and the demands of monism. Cambridge MPhil thesis, 2024.

Boyd, R. 1980. Materialism without reductionism: What physicalism does not entail. In N. Block (ed.) *Readings in the Philosophy of Psychology*. Cambridge, MA: Harvard University Press: 67–106.

Braddon-Mitchell, D. 2003. Qualia and analytical conditionals. *The Journal of Philosophy* 100: 111–35.

Brown, C. D. 2026. The meaning of monism. *Synthese* 207 (115). https://doi-org.libdata.lib.ua.edu/10.1007/s11229-026-05498-w.

Brown, C. D. 2023. Quantum computation and the untenability of a "No fundamental mentality" constraint on physicalism. *Synthese* 201: 10, URL = <https://doi.org/10.1007/s11229-022-04015-z>.

Brown, C. D. 2021. Fundamental mentality in a physical world. *Synthese* 199: 2841–60.

Brown, C. D. 2017a. Minds within minds: An infinite descent of mentality in a physical world. *Erkenntnis* 82: 1339–50.

Brown, C. D. 2017b. A properly physical Russellian physicalism. *Journal of Consciousness Studies* 24 (11–12): 31–50.

Brown, R., and Ladyman, J. 2009. Physicalism, supervenience and the fundamental level. *The Philosophical Quarterly* 59 (234): 20–38.

Burge, T. 2010. Modest dualism. In R. C. Koons and G. Bealer (eds.) *The Waning of Materialism*. New York: Oxford University Press: 233–50.

Burge, T. 2003. Qualia and intentional content: Reply to Block. In M. Hahn and B. Ramberg (eds.) *Reflections and Replies: Essays on the Philosophy of Tyler Burge*. Cambridge: MIT Press: 405–16.

Burge, T. 1982. Other bodies. In A. Woodfield (ed.) *Thought and Object: Essays on Intentionality*. Oxford: Clarendon Press: 97–120.

Burge, T. 1979. Individualism and the mental. *Midwest Studies in Philosophy* 4: 73–121.

Cameron, R. P. 2016. Do we need grounding? inquiry: An interdisciplinary. *Journal of Philosophy* 59 (4): 382–97.

Carnap, R. 1955. Meaning and synonymy in natural languages. *Philosophical Studies* 6: 33–47.

Carnap, R. 1928/1967. *Der Logische Aufbau der Welt*, Berlin: Weltkreis. Translated as *The Logical Structure of the World: Pseudoproblems in Philosophy*. Trans. R. A. George. Berkeley, CA: University of California Press, 1967.

Carroll, L. 1895. What the tortoise said to Achilles. *Mind* 4 (14): 278–80.

Chalmers, D. J. 2021. *Philosophy of Mind: Classical and Contemporary Readings*, 2nd Edition. New York: Oxford University Press.

Chalmers, D. J. 2020a. Spatiotemporal functionalism v. the conceivability of zombies. *Noûs* 54 (2): 488–97.

Chalmers, D. J. 2020b. Idealism and the mind-body problem. In W. Seager (ed.), *The Routledge Handbook of Panpsychism*. Routledge: 353–73.

Chalmers, D. J. 2013. Panpsychism and panprotopsychism. Amherst Lecture in Philosophy, URL = <http://www.amherstlecture.org/index.html>. Also in T. Alter and Y. Nagasawa (eds.) *Consciousness in the Physical World: Perspectives on Russellian Monism*. New York: Oxford University Press, 2015: 246–76.

Chalmers, D. J. 2012. *Constructing the World*. Oxford: Oxford University Press.

Chalmers, D. J. 2011. Verbal disputes. *Philosophical Review* 120 (4): 515–66.

Chalmers, D. J. 2010. *The Character of Consciousness*. New York: Oxford University Press.

Chalmers, D. J. 2004. Phenomenal concepts and the knowledge argument. In P. Ludlow, D. Stoljar, and Y. Nagasawa (eds.) *There's Something about Mary: Essays on Phenomenal Consciousness and Frank Jackson's Knowledge Argument*. Cambridge, MA: MIT Press: 269–98.

Chalmers, D. J. 2002. Does conceivability entail possibility? In T. Gendler and J. Hawthorne (eds.) *Conceivability and Possibility*. New York: Oxford University Press: 145–200.

Chalmers, D. J. 1997. Moving forward on the problem of consciousness. *Journal of Consciousness Studies* 4: 3–46.

Chalmers, D. J. 1996. *The Conscious Mind: In Search of a Fundamental Theory*. New York: Oxford University Press.

Chalmers, D. J. and McQueen, K. 2022. Consciousness and the collapse of the wave function. In S. Gao (ed.) *Consciousness and Quantum Mechanics*. Oxford University Press: 11–63.

Chalmers, D. J. and Jackson, F. 2001. Conceptual analysis and reductive explanation. *Philosophical Review* 110 (3): 315–61.

Chomsky, N. 1995. Language and nature. *Mind* 104 (413): 1–61.

Chomsky, N. 1988. Language and problems of knowledge. *Synthesis Philosophica* 5: 1–25. Rpt. In *The Philosophy of Language*, 4th Edition, A. Martinich, (ed.). New York: Oxford University Press, 2001: 558–77.

Churchland, P. S. 1996. The hornswoggle problem. *Journal of Consciousness Studies* 3: 402–8.

Coleman, S. 2015. Neuro-cosmology. In P. Coates and S. Coleman (eds.) *Phenomenal Qualities: Sense, Perception, and Consciousness*. Oxford: Oxford University Press: 66–102.

Coleman, S. (ed.) 2019. *The Knowledge Argument*. Cambridge: Cambridge University Press.

Conee, E., and Sider, T. 2005. *Riddles of Existence: A Guided Tour of Metaphysics*. New York: Oxford University Press.

Cornell, D. M. 2025. Material composition. *The Internet Encyclopedia of Philosophy*, ISSN 2161-0002, URL = https://iep.utm.edu/, 11/28/2025.

Cornell, D. M. 2016. Taking monism seriously. *Philosophical Studies* 173 (9): 2397–2415.

Crane, T. 2000. Dualism, monism, physicalism. *Mind and Society* 1 (2): 73–85.

Crane, T. and Mellor, H. 1990. There is no question of physicalism. *Mind* 99: 185–206.

Creath, R. 2023. Logical empiricism. *The Stanford Encyclopedia of Philosophy* (Winter 2023 Edition), Edward N. Zalta and Uri Nodelman (eds.), URL = <https://plato.stanford.edu/archives/win2023/entries/logical-empiricism/>.

Daly, C. 2012. Sceptism about grounding. In F. Correia and B. Schneider (eds.) *Metaphysical Grounding*. Cambridge: Cambridge University Press: 81–98.

Dasgupta, S. 2015. The possibility of physicalism. *The Journal of Philosophy* 111: 557–92.

Descartes, R. 1644/1985. *Principles of philosophy*, part two. In J. Cottingham, R. Stoofhoff, D. Murdoch, and A. Kenny (eds.) *The Philosophical Writings of Descartes, vol. I.* Cambridge: Cambridge University Press: 177–291.

Descartes, R. 1641/1985. *Meditations on first philosophy*. In J. Cottingham, R. Stoofhoff, D. Murdoch, A. Kenny (eds.) *The Philosophical Writings of Descartes, vol. II.* Cambridge: Cambridge University Press: 1–62.

Dorsey, J. E. 2011. On the supposed limits of physicalist theories of mind. *Philosophical Studies* 155: 207–25.

Dowell, J. L. 2006. The physical: empirical, not metaphysical. *Philosophical Studies* 131: 25–60.

Downing, L. 2021. George Berkeley. *The Stanford Encyclopedia of Philosophy* (Fall 2021 Edition), Edward N. Zalta (ed.), URL = <https://plato.stanford.edu/archives/fall2021/entries/berkeley/>.

Dretske, F. 1995. *Naturalizing the Mind*. Cambridge: MIT Press.

Dupré, J. 1988. Materialism, physicalism, and scientism. *Philosophical Topics* 16 (1): 31–56.

Elisabeth, Princess of Bohemia. 1643. Letter to René Descartes. Trans. J. Bennett, 2015, URL = <http://www.earlymoderntexts.com/assets/pdfs/descartes1643.pdf>.

Elpidorou, A. and Dove, G. 2018. *Consciousness and Physicalism: A Defense of A Research Program*. New York, NY, USA: Routledge.

Enoch, D. 2011. *Taking Morality Seriously: A Defense of Robust Realism*, Oxford: Oxford University Press.

Feigl, H. 1958. *The "Mental" and the "Physical."* Minneapolis: University of Minnesota Press.

Feynman, R. 1982. Simulating physics with computers. *International Journal of Theoretical Physics* 21: 467–88.

Fine, K. 2012. The pure logic of ground. *Review of Symbolic Logic* 5: 1–25.

Fine, K. 1994. Essence and modality. *Philosophical Perspectives* (*Logic and Language*) 8: 1–16.

Fiorese, R. 2016. Stoljar's dilemma and three conceptions of the physical: A defence of the *via negativa*. *Erkenntnis* 81 (2): 201–29.

FitzPatrick, W. J. 2022. *Ethical Realism*. Cambridge: Cambridge University Press.

FitzPatrick, W. J. 2008. Robust ethical realism, non-naturalism and normativity. In R. Shafer-Landau (ed.) *Oxford Studies in Metaethics*, vol. 3. Oxford: Oxford University Press: 159–205.

Foot, P. 1972. Morality as a system of hypothetical imperatives. *Philosophical Review* 81 (3): 305–16.

Fritz, P. 2022. Ground and grain. *Philosophy and Phenomenological Research* 105: 299–330.

Garfield, J. L. 2015. *Engaging Buddhism: Why it Matters to Philosophy*. New York: Oxford University Press.

Gibbard, A. 2003. *Thinking How to Live*. Cambridge, MA: Harvard University Press.

Goswami, A. 1990. Consciousness in quantum physics and the mind-body problem. *Journal of Mind and Behavior* 11: 75–96.

Guthrie, W. K. C. 1962. *A History of Greek Philosophy: Volume 5, The Later Plato and the Academy*. Cambridge: Cambridge University Press.

Guyer, P. and Horstmann, R. 2023. Idealism. *The Stanford Encyclopedia of Philosophy* (Spring 2023 Edition), Edward N. Zalta and Uri Nodelman (eds.), URL = <https://plato.stanford.edu/archives/spr2023/entries/idealism/>.

Hart, W. D. 1988. *The Engines of the Soul.* New York: Cambridge University Press.
Heil, J. 2003. *From an Ontological Point of View.* New York: Oxford University Press.
Hempel, C. G. 1980. Comments on Goodman's *Ways of Worldmaking. Synthese* 45 (2): 193–99.
Hempel, C. G. 1969. Reduction: Ontological and linguistic facets. In S. Morgenbesser, P. Suppes, and M. White (eds.) *Philosophy, Science, and Method: Essays in Honor of Ernest Nagel.* New York: St. Martin's Press: 179–99.
Hestevold, H. S. 1981. Conjoining. *Philosophy and Phenomenological Research* 41 (3): 371–85.
Horgan, T. 1993. From supervenience to superdupervenience: Meeting the demands of a material world. *Mind* 102: 555–86.
Horgan, T. and Potrč, M. 2000. Blobjectivism and indirect correspondence. *Facta Philosophica* 2: 249–70.
Howell, R. J. 2013. *Consciousness and the Limits of Objectivity: The Case for Subjective Physicalism.* Oxford: Oxford University Press.
Howell, R. J. 2012. Physicalism, old school. In T. Alter and R. J. Howell (eds). *Consciousness and the Mind-Body Problem.* New York: Oxford University Press: 337–48.
Howell, R. J. 2009. Emergentism and supervenience physicalism. *Australasian Journal of Philosophy* 87 (1): 83–98.
Hume, D. 1738. *A Treatise of Human Nature.* Oxford: Oxford University Press, 1978.
Jackson, F. 1998. *From Metaphysics to Ethics: A Defence of Conceptual Analysis.* Oxford: Oxford University Press.
Jackson, F. 1995. Postscript. In Moser and Trout (eds.) *Contemporary Materialism: A Reader.* New York: Routledge: 184–89.
Jackson, F. 1982. Epiphenomenal qualia. *The Philosophical Quarterly* 32: 127–36.
James, W. 1890. *The Principles of Psychology.* New York, NY: Henry Holt.
Jaworski, W. 2016. *Structure and the Metaphysics of Mind: How Hylomorphism Solves the Mind-Body Problem.* Oxford: Oxford University press.
Kant, I. 1781/87. *Critique of Pure Reason.* P. Guyer and A. Wood (trs.). New York: Cambridge University Press, 1987.
Kaplan, D. 1975. How to Russell a Frege-Church. *Journal of Philosophy* 72 (19): 716–29.
Kim, J. 2011. From naturalism to physicalism: Supervenience redux. *Proceedings and Addresses of the American Philosophical Associate* 85 (2): 109–34.
Kim, J. 2005. *Physicalism, or Something Near Enough.* Princeton, NJ: Princeton University Press.
Kim, J. 1998. *Mind in a Physical World: An Essay on the Mind-Body Problem and Mental Causation.* Cambridge: MIT Press.
Kim, J. 1993. *Supervenience and Mind: Selected Philosophical Essays.* Cambridge: Cambridge University Press.
Kim, J. 1989. Mechanism, purpose, and explanatory exclusion. *Philosophical Perspectives* 3: 77–108.
Kim, J. 1984. Concepts of supervenience. *Philosophy and Phenomenological Research* 45 (2): 153–76.
Koslicki, K. 2015. The course-grainedness of grounding. In K. Bennett and D. Zimmerman (eds.) *Oxford Studies in Metaphysics: Volume 9.* Oxford: Oxford University Press.
Kripke, S. 1972. Naming and necessity. In G. Harman and D. Davidson (eds.) *The Semantics of Natural Language.* D. Reidel Publishing Company: 253–355.
Ladyman, J., and Ross, D., with Spurrett, D., and Collier, J. 2007. *Every Thing Must Go.* Oxford: Oxford University Press.
Leuenberger, S. 2014. Grounding and necessity. *Inquiry* 57: 151–74.

Levine, J. 2001. *Purple Haze: The Puzzle of Consciousness*. Oxford: Oxford University Press.

Levine, J. 1983. Materialism and qualia: the explanatory gap. *Pacific Philosophical Quarterly* 64: 354–61.

Lewis. D. K. 2001. Ramseyan humility. In D. Braddon-Mitchell and R. Nola (eds.) *The Canberra Plan*. Oxford: Oxford University Press. Rpt. In D. Braddon-Mitchell and R. Nola (eds.) *Conceptual Analysis and Philosophical Naturalism*. Cambridge, MA: MIT Press, 2009: 203–22.

Lewis, D. K. 1997. Naming the colours. *The Australasian Journal of Philosophy* 75 (3): 325–42.

Lewis, D. K. 1986. *On the Plurality of Worlds*. Oxford: Oxford University Press.

Lewis, D. K. 1983. New work for a theory of universals. *The Australasian Journal of Philosophy* 61 (4): 343–77.

Lewis, D. K. 1980. Mad pain and Martian pain. In N. Block (ed.) *Readings in Philosophy of Psychology*, vol. 1. Cambridge, MA: Harvard University Press: 216–22.

Lewis, D. K. 1966. An argument for the identity theory. *Journal of Philosophy* 63: 17–25.

Loewer, B. M. 2001. From physics to physicalism. In C. Gillett and B. Loewer (eds.) *Physicalism and Its Discontents*. Cambridge: Cambridge University Press: 37–56.

Ludlow, P., Stoljar, D., and Nagasawa, Y. (eds.) *There's Something about Mary: Essays on Phenomenal Consciousness and Frank Jackson's Knowledge Argument*. Cambridge, MA: MIT.

Mach, E. 1910. *The Analysis of Sensations*. Trans. C. M. Williams, Chicago, IL: Open Court.

Malebranche, N. 1674–5/1980. *The Search after Truth*. Trans. T. M. Lennon and P. J. Olscamp. Columbus: Ohio State University Press.

Markosian, N. 2000. What are physical objects? *Philosophy and Phenomenological Research* 61: 375–95.

McKitrick, J. 2003. The bare metaphysical possibility of bare dispositions. *Philosophy and Phenomenological Research* 66: 349–69.

Melnyk, A. 2016. Grounding and the formulation of physicalism. In K. Aizawa and C. Gillett (eds.) *Scientific Composition and Metaphysical Ground*. London: Palgrave-Macmillan: 249–69.

Melnyk, A. 2003. *A Physicalist Manifesto: Thoroughly Modern Materialism*. New York: Cambridge University Press.

Melnyk, A. 1997. How to keep the "physical" in physicalism. *Journal of Philosophy* 94: 622–37.

The Milinda Pañha. Circa 100 bce–200 ce. Trans. T. W. Rhys Davids. Jazzybee Verlag: Loshberg.

Mill, J. S. 1843. *A System of Logic, Ratiocinative and Inductive*. London: Cambridge University Press.

Montero, B. G. 2015. Russellian physicalism. In T. Alter and Y. Nagasawa (eds.) *Consciousness in the Physical World: Perspectives on Russellian Monism*. New York: Oxford University Press: 209–23.

Montero, B. G. 2024. The gap in the knowledge argument. *Philosophia* 52 (2): 235–44.

Montero, B. G. 2013. Must physicalism imply supervenience of the mental on the physical? *Journal of Philosophy* 110: 93–110.

Montero, B. G. 2012. Response to Robert J. Howell's commentary, URL = <https://consciousnessonline.files.wordpress.com/2012/02/montero-response-to-howell.pdf>.

Montero, B. G. 2006. Physicalism in an infinitely decomposable world. *Erkenntnis* 64: 177–91.

Montero, B. G. 2005. What is the physical? In B. McLaughlin (ed.) *The Oxford Handbook of Philosophy of Mind*. Oxford: Oxford University Press: 173–88.

Montero, B. 1999. The body problem. *Noûs* 33: 183–200.
Montero, B. and Brown, C. D. 2018. Making room for a this-worldly physicalism. *Topoi* 37 (3): 523–32.
Montero, B. and Papineau, D. 2005. A defence of the *via negativa* argument for physicalism. *Analysis* 65: 233–37.
Moorfoot, W. 2024. Type-R physicalism. *Philosophical Psychology*. DOI: 10.1080/09515089.2024.2396019.
Morris, K. 2019. *Physicalism Deconstructed: Levels of Reality and the Mind-Body Problem.* Cambridge: Cambridge University Press.
Morris, K. 2014. Supervenience, physicalism, emergentism, and the polluted supervenience base. *Erkenntnis* 70: 351–65.
Newman, M. 1928. Mr. Russell's causal theory of perception. *Mind* 5: 26–43.
Ney, A. 2016. Grounding in the philosophy of mind: A defense. In K. Aizawa and C. Gillett (eds.) *Scientific Composition and Metaphysical Ground.* London: Palgrave-Macmillan: 271–300.
Ney, A. 2008. Physicalism as an attitude. *Philosophical Studies* 138: 1–15.
Neurath, O. 1931. Physicalism. *The Monist* 41: 618–623. Also in R. S. Cohen and M. Neurath (eds.) *Otto Neurath Philosophical Papers 1913–1946.* Dordrecht: D. Reidel Publishing Company, 1983: 52–57.
O'Conaill, D. 2018. Grounding, physicalism and necessity. *Inquiry* 61 (7): 713–30.
Orilia, F. and P. Paoletti, M. 2022. Properties. *The Stanford Encyclopedia of Philosophy* (Spring 2022 Edition), Edward N. Zalta (ed.), URL = <https://plato.stanford.edu/archives/spr2022/entries/properties/>.
Papineau, D. 2002. *Thinking about Consciousness.* New York: Oxford University Press.
Parfit, D. 1984. *Reasons and Persons.* Oxford: Oxford University Press.
Pautz, A. Forthcoming. How to achieve the physicalist dream: Identity or ground? In G. Rabin (ed.) *Grounding and Consciousness.* New York: Oxford University Press.
Pelczar, M. 2015. *Sensorama: A Phenomenalist Analysis of Spacetime and Its Contents.* New York: Oxford University Press.
Pereboom, D. 2020. Constitution, nonreductivism, and emergence. In L. R. G. Oliveira and K. J. Corcoran (eds.) *Themes from the Philosophy of Lynne Rudder Baker.* New York: Routledge: 96–113.
Pereboom, D. 2019. Russellian monism, introspective inaccuracy, and the illusion meta-problem of consciousness. *Journal of Consciousness Studies* 26 (9–10): 182–93.
Pereboom, D. 2011. *Consciousness and the Prospects of Physicalism.* New York: Oxford University Press.
Pereboom, D. 2002. Robust nonreductive materialism. *Journal of Philosophy* 99: 499–531.
Place, U. T. 1956. Is consciousness a brain process? *British Journal of Psychology* 47: 44–50.
Poland, J. 2003. Chomsky's challenge to physicalism. In L. Antony and N. Hornstein (eds.) *Chomsky and His Critics.* Oxford: Blackwell: 29–48.
Putnam, H. 1975. The meaning of "meaning." *Minnesota Studies in the Philosophy of Science* 7: 131–93.
Putnam, H. 1967. The nature of mental states. Originally entitled "Psychological predicates." In W. H. Capitan and D. D. Merrill (eds.) *Art, Mind, and Religion.* Pittsburgh: Pittsburgh University Press: 37–48.
Quine, W. V. O. 1960. *Word and Object.* Cambridge, MA: MIT Press.
Rickless, S. C. 2013. *Berkeley's Argument for Idealism.* Oxford: Oxford University Press.
Robinson, H. 2023. Dualism. *The Stanford Encyclopedia of Philosophy* (Spring 2023 Edition), Edward N. Zalta and Uri Nodelman (eds.), URL = <https://plato.stanford.edu/archives/spr2023/entries/dualism/>.

Rosen, G. 2010. Metaphysical dependence: Grounding and reduction. In B. Hale and A. Hoffmann (eds.) *Modality: Metaphysics, Logic, and Epistemology*. Oxford: Oxford University Press: 109–35.

Russell, B. 1951. *The Autobiography of Bertrand Russell 1914–1944*. Boston: Little, Brown and Company.

Russell, B. 1927. *The Analysis of Matter*. London: Kegan Paul.

Schaffer, J. 2018. Monism. In *The Stanford Encyclopedia of Philosophy* (Winter 2018 Edition), Edward N. Zalta (ed.), URL = <https://plato.stanford.edu/archives/win2018/entries/monism/>.

Schaffer, J. 2017. The ground between the gaps. *Philosophers' Imprint* 17 (11): 1–26.

Schaffer, J. 2016. Ground rules: Lessons from Wilson. In K. Aizawa and C. Gillett (eds.) *Scientific Composition and Metaphysical Ground*. London: Palgrave Macmillan: 143–70.

Schaffer, J. 2010. Monism: The priority of the whole. *Philosophical Review* 119: 31–76.

Schaffer, J. 2003. Is there a fundamental level? *Nous* 37: 498–517.

Schneider, S. 2017. Does the mathematical nature of physics undermine physicalism? *Journal of Consciousness Studies* 24 (9–10): 7–39.

Segal, A. and Goldschmidt, T. 2017. The necessity of idealism. In T. Goldschmidt and K. L. Pearce (eds.) *Idealism: New Essays in Metaphysics*. Oxford University Press: 34–49.

Shoemaker, S. 1980. Causality and properties. In P. v. Inwagen (ed.) *Time and Change*. Dordrecht: D. Reidel: 109–35.

Sider, T. 2011. *Writing the Book of the World*. Oxford: Oxford University Press.

Skiles, A. 2015. Against grounding necessitarianism. *Erkenntnis* 80: 717–51.

Smart, J. J. C. 1959. Sensations and brain processes. *Philosophical Review* 68: 141–56.

Spinoza, B. 1677/2018. *Ethics Proved in Geometrical Order*. New York: Cambridge University Press. Edited by M. J. Kisner.

Spurrett, D. 2001. What physical properties are. *Pacific Philosophical Quarterly* 82 (2): 201–25.

Spurrett, D. and Papineau, D. 1999. A note on the completeness of "Physics." *Analysis* 59 (1): 25–29.

Stapp, H. P. 1993. *Mind, Matter, and Quantum Mechanics*. Berlin: Springer.

Stoljar, D. 2010. Physicalism. New York: Routledge.

Stoljar, D. 2022. Physicalism, *The Stanford Encyclopedia of Philosophy* (Summer 2022 Edition), Edward N. Zalta (ed.), URL = <https://plato.stanford.edu/archives/sum2022/entries/physicalism/>.

Stoljar, D. 2020a. Chalmers v Chalmers. *Noûs* 54 (2): 469–87.

Stoljar, D. 2020b. Panpsychism and non-standard materialism: Some comparative remarks. In W. Seager (ed.) *The Routledge Handbook of Panpsychism*. Routledge: 218–29.

Stoljar, D. 2015. Russellian monism or Nagelian monism? In T. Alter and Y. Nagasawa (eds.) *Consciousness in the Physical World: Perspectives on Russellian Monism*. New York: Oxford University Press: 324–45.

Stoljar, D. 2014. Four kinds of Russellian monism. In U. Kriegel (ed.) *Current Controversies in Philosophy of Mind*. New York: Routledge: 17–39.

Stoljar, D. 2006. *Ignorance and Imagination: The Epistemic Origin of the Problem of Consciousness*. New York: Oxford University Press.

Strawson, G. 2008. *Real Materialism: And Other Essays*. Oxford: Oxford University Press.

Strawson, G. 2006. Realistic monism: Why physicalism entails panpsychism. In A. Freeman (ed.) *Consciousness and Its Place in Nature*. Exeter: Imprint Academic: 3–31.

Stroud, B. 2000. *The Quest for Reality*. New York: Oxford University Press.

Stubenberg, L. and Wishon, D. 2023. Neutral monism. *The Stanford Encyclopedia of Philosophy* (Spring 2023 Edition), Edward N. Zalta and Uri Nodelman (eds.), URL = <https://plato.stanford.edu/archives/spr2023/entries/neutral-monism/>.

Swoyer, C. 1982. The nature of natural laws. *Australasian Journal of Philosophy* 60: 2003–23.

Tye, M. 2009. *Consciousness Revisited: Materialism Without Phenomenal Concepts.* Cambridge, MA: MIT Press.

Tye, M. 2007. The problem of common sensibles. *Erkenntnis* 66 (1–2): 287–303.

van Cleve, J. 1999. *Problems from Kant.* New York: Oxford University Press.

van Inwagen, P. 1995. *God, Knowledge & Mystery: Essays in Philosophical Theology.* Ithaca: Cornell University Press.

van Inwagen, P. 1990. *Material Beings.* Ithaca, NY: Cornell University Press.

van Inwagen, P. 1978. The possibility of resurrection. *International Journal for Philosophy of Religion* 9 (2): 114–21.

Weisberg, J. 2025. *Explanatory Optimism About the Hard Problem of Consciousness.* Routledge.

Werner, J. 2025. Physicalism, foundationalism, and infinite descent. *Erkenntnis* 90 (2): 789–94.

Wigner, E. P. 1962. Remarks on the mind-body question. In I. J. Good (ed.), *The Scientist Speculates: An Anthology of Partly-Baked Ideas.* London: Heinemann: 284–302.

Wilson, J. M. 2021. *Metaphysical Emergence.* Oxford: Oxford University Press.

Wilson, J. M. 2014. No work for a theory of grounding. *Inquiry* 57: 1–45.

Wilson, J. M 2006. On characterizing the physical. *Philosophical Studies* 131: 61–99.

Wilson, J. M. 2005. Supervenience-based formulations of physicalism. *Noûs* 39: 426–59.

Wishon, D. 2021. Radical empiricism, neutral monism, and the elements of mind. *The Monist* 104 (1): 125–51.

Witmer, D. G. 2020. Physicalism unblocked. *Canadian Journal of Philosophy* 50: 890–904.

Witmer, D. G. 2018. Physicality for physicalists. *Topoi* 37 (3): 457–72.

Witmer, D. G. 2017. Platonistic physicalism without tears. *Journal of Consciousness Studies* 24 (9–10): 72–90.

Witmer, D. G. 2001. Sufficiency claims and physicalism: a formulation. In C. Gillett and B. Loewer (eds.) *Physicalism and Its Discontents.* Cambridge: Cambridge University Press: 57–73.

Worley, S. 2006. Physicalism and the *via negativa. Philosophical Studies* 131 (1): 101–26.

Yetter-Chappell, H. 2025. *The View from Everywhere: Realist Idealism Without God.* Oxford: Oxford University Press.

Yetter-Chappell, H. 2017. Idealism without God. In K. Pearce and T. Goldschmidt (eds.) *Idealism: New Essays in Metaphysics.* Oxford University Press: 66–81.

Zangwill, N. 2011. Negative properties. *Nouŝ* 45 (3): 528–56, URL = <https://doi.org/10.1111/j.1468-0068.2010.00776.x>.

Zhong, L. 2021. Physicalism without supervenience. *Philosophical Studies* 178 (5): 1529–44.

Zhong, L. 2016. Physicalism, psychism, and phenomenalism. *Journal of Philosophy* 113 (11): 572–90.

Index

For the benefit of digital users, indexed terms that span two pages (e.g., 52–53) may, on occasion, appear on only one of those pages.